A gift for

_____

From

_____

Date

_____

THIS IS NOT FOREVER

*Hopeful Reminders That God
Has Abundantly More in Store*

---

90 Devotions

Sarah Grace Hallas

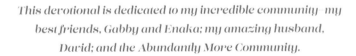

This devotional is dedicated to my incredible community—my best friends, Gabby and Enaka; my amazing husband, David; and the Abundantly More Community.

ZONDERVAN

This Is Not Forever

© 2024 Sarah Grace Lima

Published in Grand Rapids, Michigan, by Zondervan. Zondervan is a registered trademark of The Zondervan Corporation, L.L.C., a wholly owned subsidiary of HarperCollins Christian Publishing, Inc.

Requests for information should be addressed to customercare@harpercollins.com.

ISBN 978-0-310-46429-7 (HC)
ISBN 978-0-310-46428-0 (audiobook)
ISBN 978-0-310-46426-6 (eBook)

The Steffany Gretzinger quote in entry 69 is from a sermon on YouTube at https://www.youtube.com/watch?v=qAjKn98uExA.

Art direction, cover design, and art: Sabryna Lugge

Printed in Malaysia

24 25 26 27 28 OFF 10 9 8 7 6 5 4 3 2 1

Contents

Introduction

Since you're holding this book, there's a good chance that you're waving the white flag. Something has happened that makes you feel like God has abandoned you or like you've failed. Maybe you've been struggling to keep your head above water for quite some time, and you're tired of just trying not to drown. Maybe you're afraid that this hard season will last forever—and, friend, you are not alone.

My last few years have been marked by heartbreak, rejection, financial struggle, single motherhood, a depression diagnosis, and other trials I honestly never thought I'd walk through.

But here's the thing: even in my most difficult and darkest season, God opened my eyes to see His purpose through it all. He showed me His plan was so much more than I could imagine, and every difficult circumstance was preparing me to walk in that plan—not preventing me from seeing it. The Enemy wanted me to believe that hard seasons were something I deserved, or a punishment of some kind. But God allowed my own plans to fall through and took me through that time—of discouragement, doubt, redirection, waiting, and pruning—out of His kindness, to show me He had abundantly more in store.

Ephesians 3:20 tells us that God will do "far more abundantly than all that we ask or think." I don't know what that looks like for you.

But in my own life, that has meant letting go of my false sense of control and what I think should happen, and trusting that if something isn't going my way, God's preparing to do something so much better.

My prayer is that even when life seems to bring one disappointment after another, you can trust that it is not forever, and I hope this devotional encourages you to live as though your circumstances could change overnight.

I love you, friend! So glad you're here. We're in this together.

XOXO,
Sarah

1
Abundantly More

Now to him who is able to do far more abundantly than all that we ask or think.

Ephesians 3:20

In 2021, I remember sobbing, holding my newborn son, Harv, as a newly divorced single mom, asking God, "Why?!" Why was He allowing me to be in that position? What could I have possibly done so wrong to deserve it? I felt alone, and I begged God to change my situation. I remember specifically praying, "If You bring me a new husband, bless my business financially, and send someone to help me with my baby, I will give You the glory. I promise. Just please, get me out of this."

Something in my spirit then told me to open up an old journal I had kept while I was struggling in my marriage. I was afraid to open it and relive those painful memories, but I did it anyway. I flipped through journal entries detailing how alone, rejected, and abandoned I felt by my husband. Then I read, "Lord, forgive me. I've been praying and begging You to change my husband and change my circumstances, but what I think You really wanted to change this whole time was me."

The Lord began working on my heart as I shifted my focus from asking Him to change my husband to asking Him to change me. What I didn't know was that He was preparing me to walk through divorce and single motherhood less than a year later. As I read those words,

I heard God gently whisper, *Look how far I've brought you. Now trust that I'll do it again.* And it was in that moment that I remembered how much peace God gave me when my husband eventually divorced me and how much hope He gave me for the future despite my worst nightmare coming true.

By asking God to change my circumstances, I was missing out on exactly what He wanted to do in me, through my circumstances, to prepare me for what was next. Since that journal entry, the pruning and refining through difficult seasons and trials have not stopped, but the harvest has been abundant.

As we walk through this season of pruning together, as the Holy Spirit speaks to you through these pages to soften your heart and stir your spirit, I pray that you remember this: God's plan for you is so much bigger than your own. Trust His perfect preparation and plan today.

Heavenly Father, thank You for what You're doing behind the scenes right now, preparing me for what I cannot see. Honestly, I'm tired and struggling with where You have me right now. Give me hope and perseverance as You prepare me to walk in the abundance You have in store. In Jesus' name, amen.

2
The Confidence of Christ in Me

*I know how to be brought low, and I know how to abound.
In any and every circumstance, I have learned the
secret of facing plenty and hunger, abundance and need.
I can do all things through him who strengthens me.*

Philippians 4:12–13

When I was growing up, my parents would tell me that I could do anything I put my mind to. They assured me that everything I touched would turn to gold. So, naturally, anything I enjoyed doing, I did as if I were the best in the world. When I eventually read the verse from Philippians that says "I can do all things through Christ," well, of course I could!

This unbridled confidence was sometimes a great thing—it led me to create makeup tutorials as a thirteen-year-old, *with braces*, with looks inspired by a "burnt sunset." (Yes, that means I've got a very orange and red eye makeup look on the internet with hundreds of thousands of views, thanks to the confidence instilled by my amazing parents!)

But then I had a good friend who would frequently remind me, "There are actually many things you *cannot* do." She saw it as her mission to bring me back down to earth when I would convince myself I could do things that were clearly beyond my physical capability, like sing, play musical instruments, make a tasty home-cooked meal from scratch, or dance hip-hop.

She was right. There were things I couldn't do. I failed many, many times, despite my bold confidence. And when that happened, it would paralyze me. All of that confidence my parents had built would deflate. My worst nightmare would become glaringly obvious: *Maybe I'm actually not enough.*

Are you holding yourself back from attempting something that God has put on your heart because you're afraid? Is your confidence shaken because you think you're not enough?

As someone who has been there before, and as your biggest cheerleader, I want you to know that Christ in you is *enough*; therefore, *you* are enough. Your identity and worthiness in Christ change everything.

Instead of either striving to perform at a level you think you need to or failing to even try because you're afraid, can I encourage you to simply give Him your obedience? When you surrender what the outcome looks like and step out in faith, you will be amazed at what God can and will do through you.

Heavenly Father, I'm terrified of failing. And that has been keeping me from being fully obedient to what You're asking of me. Today, I surrender my desire to get it "right" every time. Instead, I plan to simply walk in the direction You are calling me. I trust that You will direct my steps toward Your perfect plan. In Jesus' name, amen.

Christ in you is Enough

3

The Birds Aren't Stressed; Why Are You?

"Look at the birds of the air: they neither sow nor reap nor gather into barns, and yet your heavenly Father feeds them. Are you not of more value than they?"

Matthew 6:26

"I have no idea what's next!"

Have you said this recently, uncertain of your future or even your next few steps? I found myself saying this many times for several years. I thought when I got married, the rest of my life would be a breeze. Then 2020 happened . . . then a divorce . . . then an unexpected pregnancy. It's safe to say not a single thing has gone the way I planned! I only started learning to trust God the way the birds of the air do purely from a place of desperation, when I was crying out to the Lord. "God, what am I doing wrong? I feel like I take one step forward just to take three back."

And then, not only did I watch Him miraculously provide for me more times than I could count, but I began to learn that sometimes when God didn't give me what I asked for, it wasn't because I didn't have enough faith. It wasn't because I didn't deserve something. It was because He wanted to teach me to surrender my desires to Him and watch Him provide something much better than I could have orchestrated on my own.

There is an abundance of evidence of the Lord's consistent, unfailing provision. I bet you can look at your life right now and recognize at least one area of answered prayer. He's promised that you will always have what you need, and He'll provide even more. Do you trust Him?

What I love about these words of Jesus in today's verse from Matthew is that they signal that the birds stay in their own lane. They're not doing what they think they're supposed to be doing or copying anyone else. They're following their own purpose and trusting God for their provision. Maybe you're seeing others pursue a certain business, ministry, or opportunity and you keep comparing your journey to theirs. Remember that there's nothing you can do to make you more "successful" than being obedient to what God has for you.

The beauty of trusting the Lord is that you can live each day with gratitude and the expectation that your needs will be met. You don't have to wait and see how the day will play out. You can be confident that even though you may not have all that you *want*, you'll have exactly what you need.

Heavenly Father, thank You for Your promise of provision. Help me to stop striving, doing all the things I think I'm supposed to be doing for my security when I just need to obey what You've called me to and trust You with the rest. Give me discernment to see clearly where You're calling me and to be a good steward of what You're given me. In Jesus' name, amen.

4

Don't Let Your Fear
Hinder Your Future

"Be strong and courageous. Do not fear or be in
dread of them, for it is the LORD your God who goes
with you. He will not leave you or forsake you."

Deuteronomy 31:6

When I was feeling particularly discouraged one day, I reached out
to my friend Katie to ask for some guidance. As she listened to me
vent about how insecure I felt about my purpose and my ability to
do what God was calling me to, she said, "Sarah, don't you realize
that the Enemy is attacking you in the same exact areas that God
has called you to empower others?" I couldn't believe it. I had let
the Enemy get me so wound up and focused on my own fear, I hadn't
taken a step back to see what was clearly taking place! I was experiencing a direct attack on the areas God wanted to use for His glory,
and this had kept me from moving forward.

If you're feeling afraid or discouraged, pay attention, because
the Enemy attacks exactly where the Lord is at work. The Enemy
knows that as soon as you stop listening to your flesh and start walking by faith, you'll see God's plan supernaturally fall into place, and
your fears will be dismissed. How is fear holding you in bondage

today? Is it fear of what someone else thinks of you? Fear of failure? Fear of being alone? Not being enough?

I want to encourage you—instead of just "praying those fears away," go to the root of those fears, and ask God to replace your fears with His truth. As you dig deep, ask yourself, *What am I really afraid of?*

When God leads you into something you can't accomplish on your own, that is an opportunity to watch Him come through for you. Instead of stressing over how you're going to make it out on your own, ask Him to equip you with exactly what you need. Not only will this increase your faith, but a deep examination of your fears and how they stack up with God's truth will carry you into the next season where you may need that insight even more.

When it's tempting to ask God to remove you from your current situation, instead ask Him how He wants to strengthen you *through* it. There's purpose in this season. The way your faith and dependence on God are developed here is crucial for what's coming next. Trust Him.

Heavenly Father, thank You for fighting my battles on my behalf and for being a source of protection and comfort I know I can trust. I want to be set free from any doubt or discouragement I've allowed to take root in my mind and my heart so I can be strong and courageous like You're called me to be. In Jesus' name, amen.

5
You Weren't Meant to Be Hidden

"You are the light of the world. A town built on a hill
cannot be hidden. Neither do people light a lamp and
put it under a bowl. Instead they put it on its stand, and
it gives light to everyone in the house. In the same way,
let your light shine before others, that they may see
your good deeds and glorify your Father in heaven."

Matthew 5:14-16 NIV

I spent about seven years working in a company where my co-workers were not Christians, and some of them didn't make the best lifestyle choices. This was a dangerous environment for me, opening doors to situations and activities I never would have otherwise considered: drinking more than I should, engaging in conversations I would've normally cringed at, and spending time with people who pulled me the opposite direction I wanted to go in life. I justified this double life I was leading—going to church while also behaving in ways I wasn't proud of—by telling myself I didn't want to be that "judgmental" Christian, making other people feel bad for their choices by not joining them. So I joined in, went along, and told myself it was all OK.

But one day when I was with someone I worked with often, I mentioned that I was a Christian, and they said, "Oh, really? I didn't know that!" I was immediately convicted, realizing that I didn't appear any different than my coworkers who didn't know the Lord at all. Here I was, thinking I was somehow being a light in the darkness, but I had really been blending in with the darkness the whole time.

You might be feeling out of place because you're a light that's trying to fit in with the darkness. Sister, as a follower of Christ, you're called to be set apart. You'll never fit in as long as you're walking in God's plan for your life. You were created to be elevated, for your light to shine and impact those beyond your own personal reach. But you can't be used if you're trying to hide.

Letting your light shine isn't about letting others see *you*; it's about letting them see God *in* you. You weren't meant to be hidden or blend in with the darkness. You were meant to be a light to the world, to show what God can do through you.

Heavenly Father, thank You for creating me with such an impactful purpose. Help me to resist the temptation to hide and instead step into what You're calling me to with boldness. Not for my own glory, but for Yours. I don't want to fit in with the dark. I want to be a light. Equip me with such an unshakable confidence in You that it radiates to others. In Jesus' name, amen.

6

Believe There's Something Better in Store

Then Pharaoh sent and called .... And when he had shaved himself and changed his clothes, he came in before Pharaoh.

Genesis 41:14

A few months after my son, Harv, was born, the Lord put it on my heart to start an online community and encourage women to walk in their God-given calling. I knew it would be a huge undertaking and a big leap of faith, but He kept giving me confirmation that this was what I was supposed to do.

So I worked day and night, around the clock. After launching the Abundantly More Community and receiving an incredible response, my excitement was short-lived. Not long after we launched, I received a message from my employer telling me that launching my community, while working with that company, was violating the terms of my employment and I would have to choose between the two. Devastated, I cried out to God through tears, "Why would You bring me this far just to leave me here?" It felt like God told me to take a step of faith but then forgot to give me the directions.

If you're feeling forgotten by God today, maybe you're wondering where you went wrong. Maybe you've been running through mental scenarios of things you could have done differently to avoid the pain and confusion. You may have even felt betrayed, like God *led* you just to *leave* you. But I believe that you're in this season as preparation, not punishment. And your situation could change overnight.

When Joseph was thrown into prison, he likely felt forgotten by God. But he faithfully served his fellow prisoners by interpreting their dreams. Two years later, Joseph was remembered by one of the former prisoners when Pharaoh needed someone to interpret his dream. As a result, Joseph was placed in a position of leadership over Egypt.

Did you catch that? Overnight, Joseph went from being in prison to being recognized for his God-given gifts and set in a place of power. This would ultimately lead Joseph to be able to rescue his people. His years in prison and in servitude were all preparation for when God would call him to a greater purpose. The difficult seasons he endured were not a punishment; they were preparation.

Although I didn't see it at the time, my difficult season was preparing *me*. Choosing to step out in faith and surrender my consistent income to start AMC as a single mom was one of the hardest things I've done, but after watching how faithfully God showed up in the midst of my trials, I knew there was a bigger purpose than I could see. This season you're in has a purpose too.

Heavenly Father, give me the strength to make it through this season. Thank You for having a better plan for my future than I could ever ask for, think of, or imagine. Give me hope when it feels like my world is crumbling down around me. In Jesus' name, amen.

GOD DID NOT LEAD YOU JUST TO LEAVE YOU

7
When the Brook Dries Up

After a while the brook dried up. . . . Then the word
of the LORD came to him, "Arise, go to Zarephath,
which belongs to Sidon, and dwell there. Behold, I
have commanded a widow there to feed you."

1 Kings 17:6-9

When life's twists and turns come my way, I handle them pretty well until . . . *I don't*. Strength turns into stubbornness. Resilience turns to resistance. Flexibility turns to fear. God will show me a shut door is part of His plan and it's not my job to force it open, but I'm blinded by my own determination.

There was a season where God was telling me to work on a certain assignment. But money was particularly tight, so instead of obeying, I spent countless hours preparing to launch a coaching program to make the money I needed, thinking *then* I'd be able to focus on the assignment. Sure enough, I launched the program I thought everyone would want and . . . *crickets*. I built so much hype, got all my systems in place, then promoted and pushed this program for weeks on end, to no avail.

I kept choosing *my* will, my own solution to the problem. Little did I know that when I finally chose obedience, God would bless me with exactly what I needed.

When the Lord limits your resources or changes your plans, it's often because He wants to lead you into something better. And the something better might be hard or uncomfortable—but it will be exactly what you need. I know your initial reaction to a change of plans may be to scramble, to try to figure out how to get everything back to the way it was or the way you think it should be. But consider the possibility that this may be an intentional move by the Lord to redirect you.

In 1 Kings 17, Elijah was called by the Lord to leave his place of comfort and go out to a new domain. God promised Elijah would be provided for there. He'd have fresh water from a brook and food provided daily. But then the provision stopped. The brook dried up.

Maybe you feel as though your brook has dried up. You feel depleted emotionally, spiritually, physically, creatively. You were following God's plan and then the plan changed. Maybe you've been angry with God, and you can't understand why things aren't working out.

You're not alone. When the brook dried up for Elijah, God was leading him to a new place where he'd be provided for. If doors are shutting or resources are running low, lean in. Keep obeying. Prepare for a miracle. God has something more in store for you.

Heavenly Father, I'm really wrestling with this season of redirection. I'm grateful for the promise of Your provision, but I'm tired. Please give me strength to keep going when it feels hopeless, and give me faith to trust Your plan for my life. In Jesus' name, amen.

8
Seek First the Kingdom

"Therefore do not be anxious, saying, 'What shall we eat?' or 'What shall we drink?' or 'What shall we wear?' For the Gentiles seek after all these things, and your heavenly Father knows that you need them all. But seek first the kingdom of God and his righteousness, and all these things will be added to you."

Matthew 6:31–33

For a painfully long season, I had just enough to live on. I lived paycheck to paycheck, often crossing my fingers that an unexpected bill wouldn't wipe the little cash I did have so I could still buy groceries that day. As a newly divorced single mom in my twenties, it was absolutely terrifying to have to trust God to meet not just my every need, but Harv's too.

But God always provided, growing my faith in ways nothing else could have. I started praying for everything! Things I wanted and needed but just didn't have the money for. And guess what? He provided. For big things, little things, and even fun things I honestly didn't think He'd care about, like a pair of jeans in my size. Now, obviously I know God isn't a genie who gives me everything I want. And yet when I allowed myself to depend on Him for my every need, it showed me just how much He cared about the little things.

What if you had so much confidence in God's provision, even if you had no idea where it was going to come from, you lived your day-to-day life with the attitude that you already have all that you need?

Jesus says that, just like the birds of the air who don't worry about where their daily provision comes from, we shouldn't worry either. "Do not be anxious" isn't a suggestion; it's a command. He will equip you with more than you need and may even give you what you want, in an even bigger way than you could imagine.

I encourage you to pray for everything—the things you need, the things you want, even the things you don't think God pays attention to—knowing that He is a great provider. But I'm begging you, don't believe the lie from the Enemy that you'll finally feel happy, satisfied, secure, confident, at peace, or content when those prayers are answered, and God gives you what you're praying for. Remember when you said that about the thing you have now? Your house, your job, your husband, your community, your kids, your health? There's always something you don't have that will rob you of your joy until you realize you have all you need in Jesus.

"Seek first the kingdom and His righteousness." Everything else flows from there. Surrender your desires to the Lord and trust that He will bring them to fruition in His perfect timing.

Heavenly Father, thank You for being my provider, my comforter, and my redeemer. Help me to remember that You see my needs and are guiding me through my current circumstances to refine me in ways that will allow me to see and pursue the things You have for me. In Jesus' name, amen.

9

It's All in His Perfect Timing

Humble yourselves, therefore, under the mighty hand of God so that at the proper time he may exalt you.

1 Peter 5:6

As I worked on this book, there were so many moments I wrestled with getting the words onto paper. My mentors kept saying, "It will happen in God's timing. The right words will come." But I still had doubts. I was new to writing a book and started writing before a book deal was guaranteed, trusting that I was being called to this for a reason.

Fast-forward to David and I getting remarried, with the final details of the book contract still up in the air. Months went by and I was continuing to write, trusting that in God's timing He would make it all "official." After weeks and months of wondering if the book deal would happen, David and I got the green light to move into our first home together as a family. We drove through the night from Florida to Nashville, Tennessee, and the second we pulled into the driveway in the U-Haul, I got the email from my agent: "It's official!" Wow. A new chapter, in every sense of the word. When I say God promotes us in *His* perfect timing, I can guarantee it won't be *yours*. It'll be so much better.

You don't have to worry about proving to God that you're worthy of that promotion or His attention, like you might have had to with that old boss or a parent. Humility will get you further than hustling ever will. Humble yourself to God and His plan. If you're called to something, God will exalt you at just the right time. So live as though your purpose is something you can live out today, not something you're waiting for. He will exalt you. It's not a matter of *if* but *when*.

God has you in this season to get you into the practice of leaning on Him for strength, while building the endurance that's necessary for the next season. Stay faithful, and you'll see God's plan brought to fruition in His perfect timing. It won't be when you feel ready; it will be when He knows you're ready.

Humble yourself. Ask Him what His plan is, and walk in faith as you prepare for it. God does not promote us like the world does. His timing is not based on appearance, experience, or preference. He seeks humility and obedience.

Share with Him the desires of your heart, and then walk in obedience to His plan, even when it doesn't look like yours. You can trust that His plan is abundantly more than you imagined.

Heavenly Father, thank You for the abundant plan You have for my life. Help me to surrender my desire to see the big picture come to fruition, and instead focus on stewarding what's right in front of me. I want to be faithful in the small things so that You can trust me with much. In Jesus' name, amen.

10
Purpose in Trial

Count it all joy, my brothers, when you meet trials
of various kinds, for you know that the testing
of your faith produces steadfastness. And let
steadfastness have its full effect, that you may
be perfect and complete, lacking in nothing.

James 1:2–4

After my son, Harv, was born, he had a hard time gaining weight. I
saw several specialists, and a lactation consultant determined Harv
was unable to properly latch and needed assistance. I was pumping, nursing, and bottle-feeding around the clock, day and night for
weeks to get him to a healthy weight. It was such a scary, lonely,
exhausting season. I remember praying, begging the Lord to remind
me, "This is not forever. There's a purpose for this season."

Trials, as tough as they are, have purpose. God might be refining
you in a specific way to perfect and prepare you for the calling He
has for you. Looking back now I can see how God used that season
in Harv's first months to shape me and form my connection with my
son in a way that I probably wouldn't have taken the time to establish
otherwise. Although this season wasn't one I would have asked for,
the joy it brought through the bond Harv and I built through the
endurance of his developmental delays has been a gift for which I
am forever grateful.

God may be leading you through a difficult circumstance today that puts you in a place where you can help someone else down the road. In my own life, God has led me through circumstances that allowed me to connect with others and bring them hope in similar situations. Whether it's through sharing a devotion in the Abundantly More Community, talking about my story on social media, or comforting a friend from church with what God did in my heart through my circumstance, there is purpose in that too.

What's robbing you of your joy today? Is it someone who's not stepping up the way you'd like them to? An opportunity you've been waiting for that hasn't happened? Have you been experiencing a long, particularly tough season? Feeling overwhelmed by too much on your plate? A lack of finances? Instead of asking, "Why is this happening *to* me?" begin to ask, "Why is this happening *for* me?"

Before God calls you higher, He might bring you low. You develop skills and wisdom in the valleys that are crucial for the mountaintops. The Bible says, "One who is faithful in a very little is also faithful in much" (Luke 16:10). Get into agreement with God's plan and lean in. This trial won't last forever. He's preparing you for some reason, and He'll equip you to endure.

Heavenly Father, thank You for the hope that my pain has purpose. Give me eyes to see Your bigger plan when I'm struggling with the trials I'm walking through. Help me to endure this time of refinement so that I can receive the fullness You have for me, lacking nothing. In Jesus' name, amen.

11

Purpose in the Pruning

"Every branch in me that does not bear fruit he takes away, and every branch that does bear fruit he prunes, that it may bear more fruit."

John 15:2

What if your current trial, disappointment, or heartbreak was preparation for something bigger than you could imagine? Something so big you would need God's power and wisdom to steward it well?

Before I could understand that in my own life, I had spent countless hours weeping, struggling to believe there was more than my immediate pain.

There were moments I never thought I'd recover from the devastation of divorce or be financially stable enough to provide comfortably for my child. But in those incredibly difficult seasons, God showed up for me in ways that strengthened my faith and refined my character more than anything else ever could. The circumstances I thought would break me were exactly what He was using to shape me. It was never a setback; it was a setup. You might not see it right now, but if you just *keep going*, I promise you will.

You can choose to walk in God's plan or your own. But you can't have both. If you want God's plan, He will be kind enough to prepare and equip you for what's next. The trade-off for His calling, though, is that it won't look like your plan. If you want your plan, that's fine!

23

You might find some immediate relief or satisfaction. You might get what you wanted for a time. But do you really want to miss out on His plan, one that is bigger than you could imagine? Do you want to miss the people He put you on this earth to impact? The changes He put you on this earth to make?

You may be exhausted by your battle because you're fighting against the very thing God is using to prune you. Pruning is essential for the purpose of growth. Your comfort is superficial and temporary, but your calling is eternal. You'll never be truly fulfilled if you're not walking in God's plan.

If there's a storm, thank Him for walking with you and ask Him what He has for you or wants from you in this season. Lean in to His plan and let Him strip you of the desire to control rather than surrender. Give up your need to strive rather than obey. You're not being pulled back. You're being prepared to launch forward.

Hearenly Father, I choose Your plan, no matter how uncomfortable it feels. I want to break free of the strongholds that are keeping me from fully surrendering to You. I rebuke the lie that my own plan coming to fruition is more important than Your purpose for me. I want others to experience the presence of the Holy Spirit through my fruit. In Jesus' name, amen.

YOU'RE NOT POWERFUL ENOUGH TO MESS UP GOD'S PLAN

12
Have the Heart of a Servant

Complete my joy by being of the same mind, having the same love, being in full accord and of one mind. Do nothing from selfish ambition or conceit, but in humility count others more significant than yourselves. Let each of you look not only to his own interests, but also to the interests of others.

Philippians 2:2–4

My best friend, Enaka, is the definition of servant-hearted. We got connected on social media through mutual friends, and we clicked right away. The week my husband served me divorce papers, she called to tell me she was thinking about moving to Nashville. The first thing out of my mouth was, "Do you need a roommate?" And the rest is history.

We had just met and moved in together a month and a half before I found out I was six months pregnant. *What? This can't be happening!*

I thought for sure Enaka would say "This isn't what I signed up for" and bounce. I wouldn't have blamed her if she had. But that's not at all what happened.

Enaka went with me to doctor's appointments, helped me build baby furniture, and even labored with me and cut Harv's umbilical cord when he was born! She helped me raise Harv as though he were her own for a year and a half, which changed my life forever. Her friendship and loyalty set the bar for the kind of friend I hope to be. She's been asked if she ever had second thoughts about loving and supporting me the way that she did, and she just says, "I felt called to do what Jesus would have done, and I know that any of my friends would have done the same for me."

What would I have done without Enaka? God had equipped her to use her gifts at the exact time when I needed them. The gaps in our lives are meant to be filled by those God puts in our path. Friends, don't withhold from others what God has equipped you with, and don't withhold opportunities for others to use their gifts to support you!

When you serve others as though you're serving God, what you pour out *will* be poured back into you. Enaka's selflessness and sacrifice toward Harv and me flowed out of her love for God and her servant heart. In turn, we added to her life and her witness of God's overflow. What an amazing display of Philippians 2 in our lives.

Do you know what your gifts are and how to use them? He will show you where and how to serve. The important thing is being willing, having an open heart to serve others. Take care of others, and God will take care of you. He's got you.

Heavenly Father, help me to trust that You see me and will take care of my every need. I don't want to spend so much time being anxious about my own needs that I miss opportunities to help meet someone else's. Give me a servant heart and show me where I am needed. In Jesus' name, amen.

13

Have Hope for What You Can't See

*For in this hope we were saved. Now hope that is
seen is not hope. For who hopes for what he sees?*

Romans 8:24

When I was a single mom, I constantly prayed for my future husband
and that the Lord would prepare my heart for marriage again. God
had been doing big work in me, helping me to trust that His plan
would be abundantly more than what I could see. So I believed and
hoped for God's best, trusting that my current circumstances paled
in comparison to His ultimate plan.

My ex-husband and I had been going through a season of mend-
ing our relationship for the sake of healthy co-parenting when he
offered to fly Harv and me down to Florida to see him for the holidays. I remember being so grateful that our relationship was on such
good terms, thanking God for doing a miracle in both of our hearts.
We flew down Thanksgiving weekend, and as I got off the plane and
saw David waiting for us, I vividly remember in that moment clearly
hearing God say, *That's your husband.*

You might be thinking, *Wow, that's so romantic! It was meant to be.*
But I'll be the first to admit it was not what I thought I wanted! God
had brought me so far as a single person, refining me, growing me—
and I thought David was part of my past, just in my life as Harv's

father. So no one was more surprised than me when it turned out my ex-husband was also my future husband!

Even in this unexpected turn of events, I could trust that it was God's best, which is exactly what I had been praying and hoping for. Little did I know that the Lord was going to use our reconciliation as a beacon of hope for others—that we'd inspire those who were looking for confirmation that God is always at work even when we can't see it. God had been preparing us separately to be used together, in a more powerful way than we could have ever manufactured on our own.

I want to encourage you today, friend. God is at work preparing a future better than you can imagine. Don't miss it because you're only looking for what fits your idea of what's best.

From what I've experienced and what I've seen in others, I can confidently proclaim: God is the author of redemption and restoration. He brings beauty out of ashes and turns mourning into joy (Isaiah 61:3). The very circumstances that seem to derail your plans can become the catalysts for God's transformative work in your life. God welcomes us to shift our focus from what we can't control to the One who holds our future in His hands. As we surrender our plans and dreams to Him, that's when we see His perfect will unfold in our lives.

Heavenly Father, thank You for being a constant source of hope and for the promise that Your plan is so much better than mine, even when I can't make sense of it. I know You are my creator and always have my best interests at heart. In Jesus' name, amen.

14
The Word Is Your Weapon

And [Satan] said to him, "All these I will give you,
if you will fall down and worship me." Then Jesus
said to him, "Be gone, Satan! For it is written,

'You shall worship the Lord your God and him
only shall you serve.'"

Then the devil left him, and behold, angels
came and were ministering to him.

Matthew 4:9–11

I often notice that what the Lord wants me to do is the last thing my
flesh wants to do. So if I find myself looking for ways to be busy, feeling overwhelmed and anxious, I know that God is probably calling
me to *rest*. In the same way, if I'm feeling stuck or unmotivated or too
tired to do something, it's pretty much a guarantee that the Lord has
something in store for me by the time I drag myself to where I need
to be. I'm becoming more aware of how my feelings can easily lead
me astray if I'm not rooted in the Word.

How often do we forget how powerful the Word of God is?
Knowledge of the Word is quite literally our strongest weapon.
Jesus was able to rebuke the Enemy in the wilderness, even in a
time of extreme vulnerability and physical weakness after fasting
for forty days and forty nights, because He knew what was written.

Right now, you may be experiencing spiritual warfare or resistance, feeling helpless or even discouraged. Remember that God has not only given you the tools to fight this battle, He's also already declared the victory.

Do you notice how the Enemy's lies are usually very close to the truth? Close enough for us to feel comfortable walking in those lies and justifying them. At times, he might even use scripture straight from the Bible, twisting God's words so that you interpret them for your own agenda. But will the things the Enemy is tempting you with satisfy your flesh more than your spirit? That's how you can recognize truth from lies, Satan's words from God's Word. The Enemy wants you to choose your comfort over your calling.

Jesus wasn't swayed by the Enemy's offers, nor did He fear that His own needs wouldn't be met. He was rooted in faith because He knew the truth of what God was calling Him to. He knew the Word of God so well He could rebuke Satan with it, fighting the Enemy on the same battleground. In the same way, we must be so rooted in the Bible that we trust His Word when our flesh fails and we're tempted to satisfy our flesh and then find scripture to justify it.

Heavenly Father, thank You for the gift of Your living, breathing Word and the power that it holds to rebuke and resist the Enemy. Help me to stand firm when my flesh is weak and I'm tempted to give in. I want the freedom that comes from knowing I'm walking in the truth. In Jesus' name, amen.

15
Walk in His Plan

I have been crucified with Christ. It is no longer I
who live, but Christ who lives in me. And the life
I now live in the flesh I live by faith in the Son of
God, who loved me and gave himself for me.

Galatians 2:20

After Harv was born, I was absolutely amazed at how all-consuming
it was to be a mom! Before I made any decision, I considered him.
Before I could do anything at all, even shower, eat, or go to the
bathroom, I had to make sure he was settled. Before making appointments of my own, I had to check to see if Harv had any. Before making
any plans, I had to see if there was anywhere he needed to be. My life
was no longer my own, and soon enough prioritizing my son became
my first thought.

When you received Christ, your plans changed. Your life was no
longer your own; you were crucified with Christ. And even now, however many days, weeks, months, or years it has been since you said
yes to Him, your life still belongs with Christ and is not your own. It
is no longer about your success, goals, promotions, and so on. It's
about walking in His plan for you so that you can be a reflection of
Him to others and live out your purpose.

Jesus died and rose again so you could have the freedom and
opportunity to walk in the fullness He has for you. You can receive

all of it or none of it. Your relationship with Him isn't one-sided, where you pick and choose when you want to trust Him and say yes. It's a two-way street built on trust and mutual love. He asks for your complete trust all the time, and then He shows Himself to be trustworthy. If you seek Him daily and get in the habit of prioritizing Him and choosing His plan over your fleshly desires, He will quickly become your first thought, and your life will radiate His goodness.

You may be tempted to go back to your old ways, your old plans, your old life. And the Enemy will tempt you with satisfaction and success. Those things can consume your thoughts so easily, right? But it's all a vapor, and it won't last nearly as long as it took you to achieve it (James 4:14). This is why the Bible instructs you to set your mind on things above (Colossians 3:2). There will always be a new distraction or source of discouragement on earth, but what God offers you will fulfill you like nothing else.

Ask the Lord to reveal to you where your flesh needs to be crucified. Slowly but surely, He will show you what you need to walk into or step away from.

Heavenly Father, thank You for the freedom I have from the bondage of my flesh. I want to declare victory over the temptation to be comfortable, and instead walk in the authority I have in Christ. I want the life You have for me, not my own. In Jesus' name, amen.

16
Your Future Is Already Written

For we are his workmanship, created in Christ Jesus for good works, which God prepared beforehand, that we should walk in them.

Ephesians 2:10

I met Hope earlier this year, and we quickly became best friends. She inspires me every day, and she has changed so many lives by simply saying yes to the Lord. With no previous event planning experience, she has thrown events with more than one hundred guests. She launched a clay earring business that quickly reached six figures even though she had no previous experience making clay earrings. And most recently, she started a nonprofit so she could give away copies of her book to women who need it!

No matter how crazy her endeavors look, she makes herself available to be used for the seemingly impossible, and this has caused many people to ask her, "How did you do that?" Sometimes they try to replicate her success. But her secret isn't opportunity, it's her obedience. She says yes to what she can do and trusts God to provide the rest.

I'm a firm believer that your faith will never return void. If you're walking by faith, you don't have to worry about the outcome or having everything figured out, because God will redirect you so that you end up exactly where He needs you. He has had to redirect me many times when I went after what I thought He was calling me toward and then the plans changed. That's OK! The problem is when God puts something on our heart, and instead of saying, "Yes, Lord, now please give me the courage to pursue it," so many of us say, "Are you sure, Lord? I don't have the courage to pursue that." We doubt Him or ourselves, or we think it's impossible.

God spent precious time making you, creating you for good works. Don't waste your life questioning His work. Instead, ask Him to empower you with exactly what you need to walk in your calling, even if it's just courage.

God has already laid out His plan for you. That's why the Bible says in Matthew 6:34 not to stress about the future: because it's already written! You have purpose. You are important. Any thought that comes into your mind that says otherwise is opposing what God has said about you, and it is a direct attack from the Enemy. Don't let those lies take root. You can simply pluck them out and rebuke them. If you want to know if there's any truth to them, ask God to reveal it to you and refine it. But don't waste your time entertaining a belief rooted in a lie.

Heavenly Father, thank You for creating me with a plan for my future that I don't need to earn or hustle for. Help me to be confident moving forward even when I don't know exactly what's next, and help me to surrender my own plan for whatever it is You have for me. In Jesus' name, amen.

YOUR
FAITH WILL
NEVER
RETURN
VOID

17
"Tell Them Who I AM"

Then Moses said to God, "If I come to the people of
Israel and say to them, 'The God of your fathers
has sent me to you,' and they ask me, 'What is
his name?' what shall I say to them?" God said to
Moses, "I AM WHO I AM." And he said, "Say this to
the people of Israel: 'I AM has sent me to you.'"

Exodus 3:13-14

When God called me to start the Abundantly More Community, I
found myself feeling like a complete imposter. I had to come face-to-
face with the fact that I had encouraged so many women to believe
that God had created them for more, and that it was their purpose
to walk in it, and yet I found myself struggling to ask—or receive—
anything but the bare minimum from God.

One day I was doing a Priscilla Shirer study that prompted me to
ask God where my faith needed to increase so that His plan could be
brought to fruition. I found myself on my knees, incredibly humbled
and honestly embarrassed by the prayer I'd been praying. It sounded
like, "Lord, I don't want more than I can handle. Just a couple hundred people in my community, and enough money to pay my bills."
In that moment I heard Him say so clearly, *Do you want to be a vessel
that overflows onto others, or one that is just barely full?* I realized in that
moment that I was letting my own insecurity and lies from the Enemy

keep me from walking in confidence of the One who supplies my purpose and power: Jesus. My fear of not being enough had blinded me and kept me from walking fully in the belief that God was enough.

What about you? Is there something God has asked of *you*? Maybe you're afraid to move forward because you don't want to be judged or ridiculed or get it wrong. Deep down, maybe you're struggling to believe that you're qualified to carry out the dream God has given you.

Sister, you're not alone.

When God called Moses to leave the sheep he was shepherding and to go in front of Pharaoh to set the Israelites free, Moses said the same thing (I'm paraphrasing): "What will they say about me?" And you know what God responded?

"Tell them who I AM."

There is an abundance you will receive in this season that has nothing to do with your talent, your strategy, or your qualifications. It's about your obedience. Surrender the desire to pursue only what you feel qualified for, and receive the invitation to walk in faith toward something that only He can equip you for. Your faith will get you further than your qualification ever will.

Heavenly Father, today I'm feeling paralyzed by the fear of what other people think of me. I want to walk in what You are calling me into with boldness, but I question my own ability and why You're calling me into this in the first place. Help me to be an encouragement to those around me to follow You. In Jesus' name, amen.

18

Don't Grow Weary of Doing Good

And let us not grow weary of doing good, for in due season we will reap, if we do not give up.

Galatians 6:9

One day I pulled up to my little mobile home at the end of a long day with groceries to bring in and unload, a sleeping toddler to put down without waking up, and a laundry list of things to do that I was already behind on. I was feeling exhausted and straight-up defeated. I had just collapsed on my couch when I looked over at the kitchen with dishes piled up and just started sobbing. The weight of doing it all on my own felt too heavy to bear. In that moment I felt God whisper, *Only once you've reached the end of yourself can you fully receive what I have for you.*

Have you ever felt this way? At the complete end of yourself? Unable to give or do anything more, while the metaphorical dishes in the sink piled up? What I've seen over and over in my toughest seasons is that God meets us at the ends of ourselves. He meets us when we've officially exhausted all our resources and backup plans and finally laid down all our pride, fully surrendered and willing to walk by faith rather than our flesh.

The pull you feel to do more, hustle harder, and be farther ahead often indicates you're trying to accomplish a dream God gave you, but in your own strength or on your own timeline. Surrender the stress, anxiety, control, and busyness that come from trying to accomplish your plan and, instead, pray for eyes to see the opportunities, provision, and support He has put in front of you today.

Paul wrote to the church in Galatia, "Do not grow weary of doing good" (Galatians 6:9, my paraphrase). What are you doing that's good? Or are you so caught up in what God isn't doing for you that you're missing what He wants to do through you? If you are planting seeds of scarcity, fear, doubt, insecurity, and shame, you will stay in that cycle and constantly reap that fruit. On the other hand, if you are sowing seeds of generosity, faith, love, kindness, forgiveness, and humility, you'll reap that fruit.

You *will* reap. But you can't give up. Don't be afraid to reach the end of yourself. Don't be afraid to go to Him and ask Him what He needs you to lay down or take action on. He will show you. Follow His voice, and you will one day see how perfectly timed God's plan is.

Heavenly Father, thank You for the promise of reaping a harvest. I pray the seeds I've been planting will reap good fruit. If I'm honest, I often grow weary, Lord. Pour out Your supernatural strength and joy today so I can continue to sow these seeds faithfully. Help me rest in Your confirmation that this season has purpose and I will soon see the fruit of my perseverance. In Jesus' name, amen.

19

Your Gifts Are Crucial to the Body of Christ

If the whole body were an eye, where would be the
sense of hearing? If the whole body were an ear, where
would be the sense of smell? But as it is, God arranged
the members in the body, each one of them, as he chose.
If all were a single member, where would the body be?
As it is, there are many parts, yet one body. . . . The parts
of the body that seem to be weaker are indispensable.

1 Corinthians 12:17–20, 22

Have you ever been jealous of someone else's gift? I have.

I cannot sing for the life of me. Like, *at all*. Now, this wouldn't be a
problem except that I love to sing. And in Nashville, I'm surrounded
by some of the most talented musicians in the world. There have
been times I've been jealous that my friends who can sing have gotten to work on fun projects together, reminding me of my glaringly
obvious lack of talent in the area I would die to have it most.

One day, as I was in worship, the Lord whispered, *They're not
operating alone.* I opened my eyes and realized that as incredibly talented as these singers were, even though they were on stage, there
were many other moving parts that went into the worship set: the
drums, guitar, tech team, piano, lights, and more!

Although my self-proclaimed jealousy is lighthearted, what the Lord impressed on my heart in that moment was my yearning for someone else's gift means I'm neglecting my own. And my gift may not mean being the star of the show, but my gift may elevate someone else and make an impact neither one of us could on our own.

Your gift, whatever that may be, is crucial to the flourishing and function of the body of Christ. The Lord grants some vision and others the gifts to walk it out.

The Enemy wants you to waste your time trying to be a different part of Christ's body so that you don't exercise the gifts that God specifically gave *you* to help fulfill His plan and complete the body of Christ. There's purpose behind your placement. And withholding your gifts because you don't feel good enough means someone else is missing out on something they need from you. Just because you don't have the gift, passion, or skills that someone else has who looks more impactful—maybe they're speaking, writing, or recording, for example—that doesn't mean your gift is unnecessary. It's actually crucial to God's plan being carried out. You are indispensable.

No one person can carry out what God has planned. We all are needed to offer the gifts He's given us to contribute to the plans He has. We were created to need each other.

Heavenly Father, thank You for creating me with a gift that is crucial to the bigger plan You have in store. Help me practice humility when asking for help and to be bold when stepping up to serve others, even when I feel unqualified or unequipped. In Jesus' name, amen.

20

Who He Calls, He Equips

I therefore, a prisoner for the Lord, urge
you to walk in a manner worthy of the
calling to which you have been called.

Ephesians 4:1

Earlier I shared about the time in my life when I had just been told that my husband wanted a divorce, and a friend I had met through Instagram, Enaka, called me out of the blue. She mentioned wanting to move away from where she lived in the DC area and possibly move to Nashville. Without a second thought I said, "Do you want a roommate? I'll move to Nashville with you!" Something deep in my spirit was ignited, and I knew this was the answer to my prayer of "What's next?" I still had no clue what that looked like, but I had the *next* step. I think back to this moment often when I'm wrestling with walking by faith, remembering to steward what I have and to surrender what I can't see.

God's plans for you will always be bigger than you. Seeing those plans come to fruition has nothing to do with your qualifications and everything to do with your obedience. He's not looking for you to be perfect or have it all together, because who He calls, He equips. So if God is tugging on your heart to step out in faith and you're questioning whether or not you're capable, you're not actually doubting yourself. You're doubting the Lord.

When I talk to women about their confidence, I usually notice one of two things. They either feel discouraged, far from where they want to be, or they're overwhelmed. They're in a season where they have opportunities they feel unequipped for or unworthy of. If you resonate with either of these, pull back the curtain on the Enemy's plan. He wants to rob you of your confidence in God's plan.

The truth is that walking in a manner worthy of your calling has nothing to do with your circumstances and everything to do with how you respond to them. If you steward what's in front of you by taking that little next step of faith rather than striving for the big, overwhelming things you can't see ahead, you'll have no doubt of whether you're worthy or equipped when doors start to open because you'll know it was His timing, not yours.

Sister, your faith will never return void. If you seek Christ and walk in faith with confidence in His plan and provision, He will redirect you if you get off track. But He can't guide you if you're standing still. Take that next step of faith with your newfound confidence in your identity and calling from God.

Heavenly Father, thank You for choosing me and placing a calling on my life. Forgive me for basing my confidence in what I can see rather than in You, the One who holds my future in Your hands. Help me remember that my confidence comes from Your ability, not my own. Please use me as a vessel for Your glory. In Jesus' name, amen.

WALK
IN FAITH
WITH
CONFIDENCE

21
Abundance Is a Promise

"The thief comes only to steal and kill and destroy. I
came that they may have life and have it abundantly."

John 10:10

When I started the Abundantly More Community, I led a live daily
devotional almost every day for years. This was a chance for me to
connect online with my growing community of mostly women in their
twenties and thirties who needed to be encouraged and who craved
community with like-minded women of faith who knew they were
made for more.

Often, just as I was about to jump on, something distracting
would happen. Or a complete lack of desire would wash over me.
At times it felt like I needed every ounce of my strength and energy
to just press Go. You know what *also* happened every single time?
Someone in the group would experience a revelation. Someone
would get confirmation of an answered prayer. Someone heard
something that brought them peace. I would get off those live videos
absolutely fired up, wishing they never had to end. I'd feel renewed
in my gifts and purpose, confirmed that what I was doing mattered.

The Enemy tries to be so sneaky, doesn't he? He's after your
gifts, talents, and passions and doesn't want you using them for the
glory of God. He wants to destroy anything that might lead to life and
abundance. But what's funny is that the Enemy always highlights

what those areas are! So the next time you feel particularly discouraged in a certain area, pay attention. That's probably where God is preparing to use you next.

Sister, abundance is a promise. It's not a question of whether or not it's available to you but whether or not you'll receive it. You may be thinking, *Girl, duh! Of course I want to receive it. I just don't know how to access it.* It's possible you're praying for doors to open and your circumstances to change, but subconsciously you're keeping yourself in the same place because it's familiar. You might be holding on to the same grudges, insecurities, unhealthy habits, and self-sabotaging and asking God to change your circumstances, when He desires to first change *you.*

As long as you have breath, you have purpose. So if you're wrestling with spiritual warfare today, that's clear confirmation that the Lord is at work. The most important thing you can do is seek Christ and posture your heart to trust Him, even when you're far from where you want to be. It's the faith that's developed in the valley that equips you to walk on the mountaintops. Don't let discouragement about where you aren't keep you from seeing where you are. Your purpose is right in front of you. You're not here by mistake. Don't miss it.

Heavenly Father, thank You for creating an abundant future for me. Help me to have hope on days where I feel discouraged for not being further along. Give me eyes to see why You have me here and what You want to do in and through me in this season. I trust Your perfect plan for me. In Jesus' name, amen.

22

The Founder of Deception

Now the serpent was more crafty than any other beast of the field that the LORD God had made. He said to the woman, "Did God actually say, 'You shall not eat of any tree in the garden'?"

Genesis 3:1

When the Lord opened my eyes and revealed to me that David was the husband I'd been waiting for—that's right, the David I had married and divorced—He followed up with so much confirmation that this was His plan for us. A couple gifted us with our honeymoon trip when they could no longer go on a vacation they had booked. David told me the name he always wanted for a daughter, and it was the same name the Lord told me my daughter would have! Truly, it was one thing after another. It was so clear to me that God was orchestrating our steps and answering my wildest dreams beyond what I could imagine.

Until the Enemy started planting seeds of doubt in my mind.

What will people think of me when they find out I went back to my ex-husband?

What if they think this is the easy road and I'm just taking it because I don't want to be alone?

What if the people supporting me in single motherhood will no longer do so?

What if people no longer trust me because my "season of hardship" is over?

I began to dread sharing this news, wishing I could keep it to myself forever.

But then I realized it was the Enemy's plan to plant seeds of fear so I'd keep my mouth shut and others wouldn't be encouraged by the reconciliation God had orchestrated! Sure enough, as I started to share, I was overwhelmed with messages from other women who were struggling in their marriages or who were single moms, telling me God's faithfulness in my own life gave them hope for what God would do in theirs.

The Enemy's plan has always been to make us question what God has said, which is what's led to our downfall since the beginning of time. In the garden of Eden, all he had to say was "Is that what God actually said?" for Eve to second-guess the truth (my paraphrase).

This is why you need time in the Word to become familiar with God's voice and character, so you can easily recognize when the Enemy is trying to lead you astray. Not everything that looks "good" is from God. Many things the Enemy disguises to appear good are actually counterfeits designed to tempt you. You need discernment to know what is *from* God and *for* you.

Heavenly Father, thank You for the Word of God that allows me to know You and know the truth. Help me not to get distracted when the Enemy plants seeds of doubt in my mind. I want to cast them out before they take root and cling to the confidence I have in Your instruction. I want Your best for me, no matter what that looks like. In Jesus' name, amen.

23
Who Hopes for What She Sees?

Now faith is the assurance of things hoped
for, the conviction of things not seen.

Hebrews 11:1

What does it mean to have hope in what we can't see? That sounds absurd, right?

Maybe it means you just got laid off, but you're believing that God's about to give you the opportunity to walk into something even bigger. Maybe it means you've walked through heartbreak, but you are choosing to believe that this absence is making room for someone even better. Maybe it means you don't know how you're going to buy groceries or pay your next bill, but you're choosing to believe that God can and will provide supernaturally, and you'll get to testify of His faithfulness.

Hope in what's not seen will never make sense to the world. So if you're starting to wonder if what you're hoping for is impossible *without* God, you're probably on the right track.

Hebrews tells us that "faith is the assurance of things hoped for, the conviction of things not seen" (11:1). Faith makes room for miracles. Faith holds space for the supernatural. Faith puts us into position to rule out nothing as impossible for God. We can only experience the fullness God has for us through faith. It's what connects what we hope and what we know.

The Lord rejoices to come through for us and bring things to fruition in a way that only He can. If you're wondering whether your faith is actually setting you up to fail, I encourage you to sit down and evaluate two things. First, what do you believe, and what do you *want* to believe? Second, what does the Bible say is true, and what are the desires of your heart? This mini self-evaluation will allow you to assess the situation with clarity so you can easily see where fear or doubt might be clouding your mind. Give yourself a ton of grace, and ask the Lord to subdue your fear and renew your hope in His plan!

The Lord wants you to have hope so you can move toward your purpose. Faith is what ignites the flame.

If you could see what God is leading you into, you might be tempted to back down—because it would feel too big or too scary. You might question your ability to be successful and prepare yourself mentally for failure. You might get caught off guard by it. God wants to do something bigger than you could imagine. So if you can't see it, try believing it. Try having faith anyway. Put your hope in God anyway. That's the only way. For whatever reason, He's not allowing you to see what's next, but this moment of not knowing won't last forever, and you can be preparing yourself for what's to come.

Heavenly Father, thank You for the hope I have in You and that I can rest knowing that even if I can't see the road ahead, You're making a way for a better future than I could imagine. Help me to trust You in the depths of my heart and to have courage to believe in what feels impossible. In Jesus' name, amen.

24

His Abundance Blesses Others

And Elisha said to her, "What shall I do for you? Tell
me; what have you in the house?" And she said, "Your
servant has nothing in the house except a jar of oil."
Then he said, "Go outside, borrow vessels from all
your neighbors, empty vessels and not too few."

2 Kings 4:2-3

When Harv and I got the news that we could move into our new little
mobile home, my excitement was quickly met with the stomach-
dropping realization that I had no furniture, no organizing containers,
nothing. I had sold it all when I thought I was moving out of state. All
I had was Harv's portable crib. Any extra money was going straight
toward moving in. Still, I prayed, asking God to provide the furniture
the same way He'd provided us a place to live.

Sure enough, when I announced my move on social media, several people asked if I would start an online wish list so they could
help support me. I kid you not—my little home was *full* of boxes with
necessities sent from people all around the world. I was completely
overcome, but not surprised, at how abundantly the Lord poured
out for me.

The purpose for your season of need is not just for you to learn
something. It's also so that others can see God come through for
you, maybe even in ways they've been praying for in their own lives.

The story in 2 Kings about Elisha and the widow radically changed my life. I heard it first in a finance class taught by my friends Bob and Linda Lotich, and I remember God immediately convicting me that the time I had been spending in fear and anxiety about my provision could be used to ask boldly for an abundance that could be used to bless others too. Long story short, the widow needed money to pay her debts, and Elisha gave her instructions, then told her to bring her children with her to witness the miracle God would do through her obedience to provide abundantly more than she needed for her family. God loves to put us in positions to witness His power and His supernatural provision, not just as a way to grow our faith but the faith of others.

When God provided all that Harv and I needed during our big move, it was a chance for my friends and family and online community to witness His abundant provision. I received so many messages from those who had been praying for us. As they watched God come through for Harv and me, they had hope He would do the same for them.

Heavenly Father, thank You for always making a way when it looks like there is no way. Forgive me for losing hope when I can't see Your provision. Thank You in advance for how You're using me as a vessel. Help me to see what You have given me and how I can steward that to bless others and give You the glory. In Jesus' name, amen.

25
Take the Next Step of Faith

Then I said to them, "You see the trouble we are in, how Jerusalem lies in ruins with its gates burned. Come, let us build the wall of Jerusalem, that we may no longer suffer derision." And I told them of the hand of my God that had been upon me for good, and also of the words that the king had spoken to me. And they said, "Let us rise up and build." So they strengthened their hands for the good work.

Nehemiah 2:17–18

Failure is my worst nightmare, so whenever I do something new, my first instinct is to make sure everything is lined up before I take my first step. It's been hard for me to learn to *just take the first step*— especially when it doesn't make sense. The problem is that walking by faith means you have to take action when God tells you to, not when you feel ready. So as much as I want to line everything up to make it perfect, walking by faith requires life to be a bit messy.

I eventually had to reach a point where I realized that instead of waiting for what's next, I had to walk *expectant* of what's next. I couldn't wait for it to all make sense or feel right; I had to expect God to cover my weaknesses, to take care of my failures. I had to let my faith dictate what I did next instead of my fear.

God wants you to take action on something with what you have right now, which is why the Enemy is trying so hard to get you to focus on what you *don't* have, to keep you stuck. God first gives the vision, then the provision. Not the other way around.

Take Nehemiah, for example, who worked his way up to a noble position as cupbearer to the king, only to have the Lord soften his heart toward rebuilding Jerusalem. Although it was a totally foreign assignment for him, he prayed, asked the king for provision, and walked through that open door with confidence that, if God were to change his heart and provide the next step, it was a step worth taking. And look at the result: God continued to fling doors wide open and confirm that Nehemiah was in the right place.

You have no idea how God is working behind the scenes to bring you the resources, provision, or support you need to bring your vision to life. Don't let fear of the unknown keep you from walking by faith. Just take the next step.

Heavenly Father, thank You for the gift of Your vision. Help me to not get discouraged when I feel like I'm the only one who sees it. I want to be the kind of woman who leads with confidence and also sparks courage in others to use their gifts. Give me the wisdom to see where You're calling me, even if it's a small step forward. In Jesus' name, amen.

JUST
TAKE
THE
NEXT
STEP

26

Don't Lean on Your Own Understanding

Trust in the LORD with all your heart, and do not lean on your own understanding. In all your ways acknowledge him, and he will make straight your paths.

Proverbs 3:5–6

After my husband and I divorced, I found myself deeply desiring a partner. So I spent time on dating apps, I met some great guys, and I even went line dancing with a group from church to meet people with similar interests. But . . . *nothing.* Nada. Zilch. *Why was dating so hard?* I found myself desperately trying to fulfill this deep desire, when I finally realized I was making marriage an idol.

Instead of answering my prayer, God called me to a place of contentment in my singleness. I was so confused—even scared!—that God would call me to be single forever. That wasn't part of my plan. My marriage might have been over, but surely I wouldn't have to do life alone. . . . *Right, God?*

Over time, as I surrendered that desire for marriage to God, I found myself praying more intentionally for my ex-husband, David. What I didn't know then was that he had been praying for me too. Eventually, God softened my heart to let David back in, something I thought I'd never do. Now I'm walking in the most beautiful redemption story, something the Lord had planned all along.

"Trust in the LORD with all your heart, and do not lean on your own understanding" (Proverbs 3:5). When I started trusting the Lord with the unknown future and His plans for my life, I never could have predicted the amazing outcome. God's plans were so much bigger and better than my own understanding.

Maybe today you're wrestling with the how, the when, or the why. Can I encourage you? God is trustworthy. He is reliable, and He is able. You can trust that where you are, and what He's called you to, are not mistakes. My season of singleness was not a mistake—it reminded me of my great need for God. Sometimes limited resources or unanswered prayers are meant to draw us near to the Lord so that we'll seek Him as our provider and comforter. If you're in this place, God might be equipping you for something much bigger or different from what you had imagined, but in order for you to fully receive what He has, you have to fully trust His plan.

If it's hard for you to trust Him today, don't run from Him. Get to know Him. If you seek Him, He will reveal Himself to you.

Heavenly Father, I admit that I have a hard time trusting You when the paths You prepare for me don't look like my own. Increase my faith, Lord. Help me walk by faith so that I can step outside of my comfort zone and experience the plans You've set before me that are so much bigger than I can even imagine. In Jesus' name, amen.

27

When You Don't Feel Like Choosing Joy

*This is the day that the LORD has made;
let us rejoice and be glad in it.*

Psalm 118:24

I have a good friend named CC who embodies joy so beautifully. Joy radiates from her in a way that's contagious. If you were to ask her why she's so joyful, she wouldn't talk about all the reasons she has to be happy, but rather all the reasons she has to be *grateful* in the midst of uncertain circumstances. Joy isn't about what you have. It's about trusting God with what you don't.

Are you choosing joy today?

To those who feel that choosing joy isn't coming easily today—and also those who want to throw this book at the thought of being told to choose joy—I promise, I won't tell you that!

The Lord woke you up today for a purpose. That purpose has nothing to do with your circumstances and everything to do with your faith. I know it's easy to look around and feel like if we're not where we want to be, we've failed, right? On top of that, there's probably something or someone you feel is responsible for your not being where you think you should be, and that's robbing you of any trace of joy you could possibly find in this season.

It's so easy to get stuck in the cycle of "This isn't what I thought the holidays or marriage or pregnancy or business would look like." It's tempting to drown in the vicious cycle of "I wish." I slip into it all the time, because I'm human. But you know what keeps me from drowning in self-pity and the narrative that "things should be different"? What makes the difference is deciding that I can choose what I do with the day the Lord gifted me.

The trials are exhausting. The hardship hurts. The struggle is real. Maybe you're fully aware that you're walking in spiritual warfare because of the calling the Lord placed on your life. Maybe you feel like the Enemy has taken everything. What brings me hope is the truth that God always has the final word. And you know what the Enemy can't take from you? God's plan.

Your pain, hurt, and disappointment are valid. You don't have to just slap a Jesus bandage on and "choose joy." But I encourage you to call out and rebuke the Enemy's assignment to discourage you or to keep you from moving forward. God never said the battle would be easy, but He did say He'd equip you for it. So why don't you ask Him to?

Heavenly Father, thank You for waking me up today. Help me to find my joy in You when I feel weighed down by the chaos and uncertainty of life. I'm grateful for the abundant future You have for me. In Jesus' name, amen.

28

Commit Your Work to the Lord

Commit your work to the LORD, and
your plans will be established.

Proverbs 16:3

When you commit your work to the Lord, you're believing that God is working all things together for good (Romans 8:28) and that He's preparing you for something bigger than you can imagine—even when it doesn't look or feel that way in the moment.

For me, committing my work to Him when I didn't feel like it meant trusting that God would prepare a way, even though I was at my lowest. I came to believe that if I stayed focused on stewarding what He'd given me, I wouldn't have to worry about what I didn't have.

For instance, one evening I had zero dollars in my bank account, but I didn't let that stop me from showing up and leading Bible study—and sure enough, someone sent me exactly the amount I needed for the bills that were due soon.

Friend, I know what it's like to feel discouraged even when you're staying faithful, especially when you aren't seeing any breakthroughs or answers to your prayers. Today's scripture says your plans will be established; it doesn't say the journey will be easy. As the mom of a toddler, many of my days are spent with my flesh being tested. My patience, self-control, peace . . . yep, all the fruits of the Spirit are tested! But as I look at my little one through the lens of my assignment, recognizing that the plans for Harv's life are bigger than his behavior in this moment and that God put me in place to prune him, my perspective changes. I no longer feel like another meltdown of his (or let's be honest, mine) will send me over the edge. I no longer feel like a failure as a mother. I have a peace that as long as I stay faithful, taking a second (or a day) to myself as I need it, I will one day see the fruit of my labor as I commit to raising my son to the Lord to the best of my abilities.

Choosing to stay faithful doesn't mean you won't get discouraged. It means you'll walk as though what you need is already taken care of—because you know that it is! Trust that the Lord will direct the outcome of your work according to His will. That outcome may not look exactly the way you wanted or planned, but you can have peace knowing He's "establishing" your desires in accordance with His.

Commit your work to the Lord. Invite Him in. Ask Him for guidance, and walk according to His plan. He'll equip you for an impact bigger than you imagined.

Heavenly Father, thank You for establishing the plans for my life. I want everything I do to point others to You. Help me to seek You and surrender my plans for Yours. I don't just want to be known as a follower of Christ; I want to be known as one who lives for Christ. In Jesus' name, amen.

29
He Has Good Plans for You

For I know the plans I have for you, declares the LORD,
plans for welfare and not for evil, to give you a future
and a hope. Then you will call upon me and come and
pray to me, and I will hear you. You will seek me and
find me, when you seek me with all your heart.

Jeremiah 29:11-13

I wonder where you might be feeling weak today. Where are you feeling like your prayers are unanswered? Maybe you have a newborn and haven't slept in months. Maybe you're rushing to meet a deadline. Or perhaps your finances are far from where you want them to be. Sister, you're certainly not alone. I, and countless other women I've talked to, often find ourselves in the same places.

Honestly, there have been many seasons where the answered prayers overwhelmed me just as much as the unanswered ones. Opportunities felt like more of a *weight* than a blessing! And my focus on the lack of provision prevented me from seeing where God was providing.

The area where you're feeling most unworthy is a clear indicator of where God wants to use you. He might not elevate you where you feel most confident or capable of succeeding, because then you might be tempted to rely on your own strength. I believe it's His kindness to show you that His abundant plans for your life don't require you to strive, hustle, or burn out. Instead, He's bringing you far enough outside of your comfort zone for you to shift your eyes toward heaven and ask for His help.

Sister, can I remind you that God didn't put you in this season to "figure it out"? He's not rolling the dice with your life, unsure of what's coming next. He knows the plans He has for us, and all we have to do is obey. Release the expectation that you have to know exactly what's next or you need to have exactly what you think you need in order to move forward. Seek Him and ask for faith to move forward. It's not the outcome God needs our obedience for. It's the surrender to the journey so He can prepare us for the outcome.

Since we know that God's plans are to prosper us, not to harm us, we can be confident that what hasn't worked out in the past is because God has something *better* for us. Lean in to wherever you feel discouraged and rebuke the lie that you are not enough. You're actually the *perfect* person for the job, and the Enemy doesn't want you to find that out.

Heavenly Father, thank You for the assurance that You hold my future in Your hands. When I'm feeling unqualified or discouraged by my lack of progress, please help me lay down my own plans to see Yours. Teach me to seek You wholeheartedly, knowing that You will guide my steps and give me hope for the future. In Jesus' name, amen.

30
The Battle Has Already Been Won

What then shall we say to these things? If God is for us, who can be against us?

Romans 8:31

Recently, I had one of those days. I woke up late, I spilled my coffee, my bag caught on the door handle on my way out, I forgot to take my meds, I forgot to put Harv's shoes on him, and I got stuck in traffic before an important meeting. In that moment, I almost reached my breaking point. I thought, *Why is all this happening to me? What else could go wrong?*

And then I remembered that I'm on an assignment that makes the Enemy upset. He doesn't want me walking in my calling, he doesn't want me encouraging others, and he definitely doesn't want me to have joy along the way. I had a decision to make: I could play the victim, or I could say, "If God is for me, who can be against me?" So I resolved not to let the Enemy's tactics distract me from the mission God has set before me.

If you responded to your biggest area of hardship right now with the mindset *If God is for me, who can be against me?* how would that shift things for you? Would you take back your power from the person you've been blaming? Would you walk with a little more boldness, knowing nothing anyone says is going to get in the way of God's plan for you? Would you be kinder to the person who doesn't deserve it, knowing their battle isn't actually with you but with the Lord?

God has the final word, and nothing you've done or walked through has hindered God's plan. So what you perceive as attacks or roadblocks are not actually preventing you from walking in what God's calling you to at all, but preparing you for it. The Lord loves to use us to display His strength. Allowing others to witness both our struggles and our deliverances is proof of His power and will lead others to Him. You just have to be willing to be brought low so you may also be raised up.

God led me on a journey that carried me through my rock bottom to walking in the fulfillment of my wildest dreams. Your valleys are crucial preparation for what's next.

Heavenly Father, thank You for reminding me that the battle has already been won and the Enemy has already been defeated. Help me to find comfort in Your power when I feel discouraged by the struggle and question my own strength. Use me as a vessel, Lord. I want my confidence in You to ignite faith in others around me. In Jesus' name, amen.

THE
BATTLE
HAS
ALREADY
BEEN
WON

31

Renew Your Mind

Do not be conformed to this world, but be transformed by the renewal of your mind, that by testing you may discern what is the will of God, what is good and acceptable and perfect.

Romans 12:2

I've watched so many people—at church, in the Abundantly More Community, even some of my closest friends—who are clearly called and equipped by the Lord and yet back down from an incredible blessing because they didn't feel qualified. *And* . . . I've also been that person.

When God revealed to me that David was going to be my husband (again), my first response was to think about all the reasons it wouldn't work, why it shouldn't happen, and why I wasn't deserving of his love. I have a note in my phone literally going back and forth with myself—almost like a conversation between my flesh and my spirit—on why reconciliation would be the best, and worst, thing ever. Of course, my heart was excited, but my flesh wanted to protect itself, and I had to seriously ask God to change my heart so my fear wouldn't speak louder than my faith in His perfect plan.

When a door is wide open in front of me, it's so easy to talk myself out of walking through it. I can throw out every reason why I'm not ready. Not capable. Not deserving. The Lord has had to seriously convict me and work on my heart for me to recognize that an open door isn't just an "opportunity." It's usually a call from Him, especially if it's something I *don't* want to do. For me, the renewing of my mind is a constant reminder that nothing God calls me to is intended to be carried out in my own strength, and all I need is for my faith to be louder than my fear.

You're not called to live according to the expectations or limitations that the world has set. The world will say, "Are you qualified for that? Are you sure you want to take that risk? Why step out of your comfort zone when you don't know exactly what's next?"

Expect to be tested. It's through testing that you draw more near to Christ and identify His voice more clearly. Often the hardships we walk through are when God is removing an idol from our lives so that He can intentionally grow us and our faith, and so we will cling to no one and nothing but Him. And the reason God calls us to go to war in prayer isn't always to change the person we feel led to pray for; sometimes it's to change *us*. Through the change we allow the Lord to do in us, we become a testimony of God's faithfulness—and that inspires transformation in others.

Heavenly Father, I want to be renewed and transformed so that every area of my life points back to You. Help me look to You as my ever-present help, instead of looking to the world for validation or guidance. I want to be a light in the darkness. In Jesus' name, amen.

32
The Truth Will Set You Free

So Jesus said to the Jews who had believed him, "If you abide in my word, you are truly my disciples, and you will know the truth, and the truth will set you free."

John 8:31-32

It's almost comical how easy it is for me to feel like I need *more*. If I have no idea what's next, I get anxious, wanting more answers. But if I suddenly have a ton of things on my plate—the opportunities I've been praying for—then I'm overwhelmed, feeling like I need help or even to step back because I'm unqualified.

In a particularly busy season—while running my business, figuring out childcare for Harv, and experiencing frequent car breakdowns that required lots of time and energy—I remember going to the Lord and asking Him to take it all away. *Lord, it's all too much! I thought I was walking in Your will, but there's been roadblock after roadblock, and I just want to give it all up and be done.* I was throwing a total pity party, wondering why everything had to be a struggle. That's when the Lord corrected and convicted me, reminding me that He would equip me for every single thing He had called me to. And if I felt like He hadn't, I needed to release control and allow Him to.

The lie I was tempted to believe was that I was unprepared or unqualified. But the truth is that I was created for good works so that I can walk in them. Not strive, not fight, not beg; *walk*. Sister, you don't need to be perfect to do good works. If anxiety or overwhelm are keeping you from acting in obedience to the opportunities God is giving you, you will take on a burden you don't need. You will be bound to a false sense of your purpose. Maybe you're already familiar with Jesus' words: "You will know the truth, and the truth will set you free" (John 8:32). But maybe today you're wrestling with what that truth even is, or how to be set free because you feel like you've been fighting for a long time and just want some hope.

God's truth is what sets us free. Anyone can hear the Word or claim Jesus as their Savior, but do you *abide by* His Word? Abiding means to endure. To remain steadfast. To not be easily swayed by what can be perceived as the easier or "better" option, clinging tightly to the hope that God will come through on His promises. That's what sets you apart and gives you access to the fullness He has for you. If you want to be set free, get in the Word and truly live by it.

Heavenly Father, I want to abide in Your Word. I want Your truth to take root in my heart and cast away the seeds of lies that are prohibiting my growth. I want to be known not just as a follower but a disciple who points others to You. Equip me, Lord. In Jesus' name, amen.

33

Pursue Obedience Before Deliverance

I want you to know, brothers, that what has happened to me has really served to advance the gospel.

Philippians 1:12

I never thought I'd say this, but I'm grateful that walking through divorce, and the hardship that followed, forced me to rely on God and gave me a tangible understanding of how good He is. Because I experienced His faithfulness through the darkest season of my life, I've been able to relate to so many more women who feel hopeless in their situation. If you had asked me years ago if I would be willing to walk through divorce to advance the gospel, my honest answer probably would have been no. But being on the other side, and seeing how many women have been encouraged to seek God in the midst of their heartbreak, I'd do it all over again.

Is what's happening to you serving to advance the gospel? Or are you spending so much time being discouraged in this season that you're missing how God wants to encourage you and use you to impact others through it?

Paul is a convicting example of what it looks like to be faithful and obedient even when it doesn't make sense. His joy was so radiant in prison that even the guards and his cellmates came to

Christ. There's a reason you're right where you are instead of further along—and it's not because you haven't done enough! It's because you're perfectly positioned for your assignment to serve someone right in front of you. Are you pursuing Christ through your season of trial, or are you pursuing a way out?

Can I tell you, sister, that your story, exactly the way it is, is what God wants to use to advance the gospel? Not the cookie-cutter version. Not the one where you didn't make mistakes. Or lose your faith along the way. Or find your identity in your accomplishments. It's the one where you surrender your plan for the Lord's, asking Him to heal your heart and fill the empty spaces with His love, even if that story starts today. Start sharing what God is doing in your life so that others may see Christ through you. Perfection isn't what makes an impact. It's struggle, trials, and hardship that unite us all.

Don't miss an opportunity to be obedient in what you're praying for deliverance from.

Heavenly Father, thank You for giving me a bigger purpose than the problems I'm facing. Help me to keep my eyes on You so I'm not discouraged by how far I feel from the life I thought I'd have. Refine the desires of my heart until they look like Yours, and give me joy in the depths of this valley. I want others to see You through me. In Jesus' name, amen.

34
Don't Block Your Blessings

*Let us then approach God's throne of grace with
confidence, so that we may receive mercy and
find grace to help us in our time of need.*

Hebrews 4:16 NIV

Do you ever feel like when it comes time to serve, attend an event like
a Bible study, participate in community groups or church, or glorify
God in any capacity, you conveniently lose your energy and desire to
show up? You can suddenly name every reason in the world why you
shouldn't go, even when you know it is something God wants you to
do. This happens to me often.

For a while, I justified staying home because I was a single mom
and needed to "preserve my energy." At other times, I felt like maybe
I had said yes to too much in the first place, so maybe God wanted
me to stay home and rest. Both reasons are certainly valid and can
be true. But sometimes we are quick to make excuses, justify our
own desires, or, frankly, take the easy way out. The next time you're
feeling "too tired," I want you to ask the Lord to reveal to you whether
you're actually being called to rest or are just relying on your own
strength.

If God is calling you to serve, and it's the last thing you want
to do, call upon Him and ask Him to fill you with His strength and
His Spirit! Ask Him to increase your capacity so that you can be an

extension of Christ and the physical hands and feet of Jesus even when you are running low. Don't let the Enemy convince you that you don't have enough to give.

You will receive the benefit of an increased capacity when you use it to serve. If you are walking in obedience, asking God to fill you and pouring yourself out to the places He has called you, you don't have to worry that you will be left empty! He will not let you run dry.

Don't neglect your call to serve and bear the burdens of your brothers and sisters in Christ. If you don't have enough to give, ask for more. He'll use you to fill others, and He'll also use others to fill you. So don't block your own blessing of being filled by the Lord or withhold someone else's blessing of using their gifts to serve Him by serving you.

Heavenly Father, forgive me for the times I don't give my time, energy, or resources because I don't feel like I have enough. Help me to ask and believe for an increase in the areas I feel called to give and to not withhold what I have out of fear. I want to receive the fullness You have for me and not block my own blessings. In Jesus' name, amen.

35
A Season for Everything

For everything there is a season, and a
time for every matter under heaven.

Ecclesiastes 3:1

I can't tell you how many times God has told me to do something, and
I brush it off because I don't feel "ready." I even justify it by convinc-
ing myself that it was just *my* idea, not something God called me to
do. Because deep down . . . *I'm afraid.* It doesn't take long before I'm
on my hands and knees before God, and time and time again I hear
Him say, *Go back and do what I told you to do.* Sure enough, every time I
go back to that thing He told me to do—days, weeks, or even months
earlier—it leads right to the thing I'd been praying for. Everything
I'd been trying to accomplish in my own strength, striving after and
stressing over to no avail, falls into my lap. And it suddenly makes
perfect sense why all the previous doors were shut.

There's a season for everything. A time to sow, a time to prune,
a time to water, a time to harvest. Every single season is necessary.
No one is less important than the others. If you're not in the harvest
season yet, you're in a season where the work you do is absolutely
crucial in preparing for it.

A tree that looks dead in the winter hasn't failed; it's actually
doing exactly what's required to bear fruit in the spring. Stop judging
your success or value based on your current circumstances, when

you have no clue what they're preparing you for! Abundance may be just around the corner.

The Enemy wants you to be so discouraged or distracted with where you are now that you miss out on the assignment God has specifically for you in this season. There may be a neighbor, a friend, a coworker, or a total stranger who needs to hear your story and experience God through you. Maybe the Lord is leading you through something that isn't crucial to your own story. Maybe He wants you to pass on the hope you received to someone else who doesn't know Jesus. Perhaps the hope you pass on will change their whole life.

Your dreams, desires, and goals matter. God created you with them and will bring them to fruition in due time, as He aligns your heart with His. He loves you too much to let you receive the fullness He has for you without being properly equipped. Trust His character and that His timing is absolutely perfect, and one day you'll see exactly how it's all working together.

Heavenly Father, it can be tempting to feel like I'm a failure when I'm not walking in the dreams and desires I have, or what I see other people experiencing. Thank You for helping me to have joy even in the seasons where I'm planting, being pruned, or being prepared for the harvest. In Jesus' name, amen.

THERE IS A SEASON FOR EVERYTHING

36

"All Things Work Together for Good"

We know that for those who love God all things work together for good, for those who are called according to his purpose.

Romans 8:28

When I found out I was six months pregnant, my life was chaos. Doctors made me feel scared that Harv wouldn't be healthy because I hadn't had medical care the entire pregnancy. The birthing center I wanted to use wouldn't take me as a client because there was no way for them to know my exact due date. I was even told that, based on my blood type, I needed a certain shot or my body might try to "protect itself" from my baby! It was a mess. But, God. Living in a new city, far from family, I watched Him send a community to rally around me and meet my every need, reminding me that I wasn't alone in the midst of this storm.

The same is true for you: you're not alone. God is still working out His plan. When you're looking at your own life and feel tempted to doubt, remember that you're still in the middle of your story.

Where does your confidence come from? Is it in your circumstance or in God? In Philippians 4:12–13, the apostle Paul wrote, "I have learned the secret of facing plenty and hunger, abundance and need. I can do all things through him who strengthens me." Our confidence should never be founded on our own ability or in our circumstance, which could change any minute—but in God's character. Do you truly believe that God will work all things together for your good?

God's purpose may be entirely different than yours. My pregnancy wasn't in my plan. But neither were the surprising community and overwhelming support that came next. Are you willing to set aside your pride and trust that God has more in store? When your faith is louder than your fear, God can move in supernatural ways beyond anything you could ever comprehend.

You can have confidence that God is working all things together for your good.

Heavenly Father, help me to obey even when it doesn't make sense or doesn't feel like it's for my "good." I know You work all things together for my good, even if I won't see it until heaven. I trust You. In Jesus' name, amen.

37

Let Your Faith Be Stronger Than Your Fear

When I am afraid, I put my trust in you. In God, whose word I praise, in God I trust; I shall not be afraid. What can flesh do to me?

Psalm 56:3-4

As I wrote earlier, when my husband, David, and I reunited, I was at peace and overjoyed at the Lord for orchestrating such a beautiful reconciliation. But deep down I was terrified for other people to find out. The Enemy had fed me a lie that because my platform was built as a single mom, people would no longer want to hear what I had to say. Or worse, they would accuse me of lowering my standards by going back to the person I had walked through so much heartbreak with.

Praying that the Lord would break those chains of guilt and shame, I gathered my courage and shared our story on social media. What happened next humbled me beyond belief. People started responding, saying their faith was increased and their hopes for their own reconciliation were restored because of what God had done in our marriage. *Wow.* Of course the Enemy wanted me focused on my fear; he knew that my step of faith would ignite the faith of others.

Fear doesn't mean you're a failure; it means you're human. What sets you apart, though, is how you respond to it. You can walk in the fullness God has for you, and this isn't dependent on your perfection or success, but your faith. Responding with fear means you've judged a situation based on what your flesh can comprehend. Responding with faith means you trust that because God's plan is beyond your comprehension, so will be His deliverance.

It's only when we've completely surrendered our plan, and clung to the Lord's, that we develop a deeper level of faith and experience a richer supply of abundance than would ever be possible in our own strength.

When everything around you seems to be falling apart, what can you cling to? The Word. His Word is truth. It's unwavering. It's empowering. It's filled with stories of people like you and me overcoming. His Word is what you can cling to when you are afraid, because it equips you to rebuke fear and walk in authority. The truth is if we trust in God, we have no reason to be afraid.

If we are praising God, we can't be paralyzed with fear. Which will you choose?

Heavenly Father, thank You for being my source of peace when I'm so far outside of my comfort zone. Help me to claim authority over my flesh when I'm tempted to be paralyzed by fear. Please increase my faith so I can walk in the fullness You have for me. In Jesus' name, amen.

38

Prayer Is the Best Preparation

Then the king said to me, "What are you requesting?" So I prayed to the God of heaven.

Nehemiah 2:4

I hate asking for help. In fact, I don't even know how to ask for help. Growing up incredibly independent, and often looking after my seven younger siblings, I was used to being in control and tending to the needs of others but rarely my own. This has made it difficult to release control and trust others, especially when it comes to asking for what I need. I've often wrestled with feeling like I shouldn't ask because I don't want to "bother" someone or come across as admitting defeat.

Maybe you also have a hard time asking for what you need. You may feel like a burden, or even like you'll be judged for not having it all together. Can I encourage you to let the story of Nehemiah give you permission to go to God with your questions, rather than beat yourself up for not having all the answers?

Nehemiah—as we discussed earlier—was a cupbearer to the king before God put it on his heart to embark on a new journey: rebuilding the broken-down walls around the city of Jerusalem. He had worked for years to reach the position of cupbearer but was being called *out* of his comfort zone, majorly. It probably wasn't his first choice, and it definitely wasn't what was most comfortable. But rather than reject it or run, he prayed. He asked God for the direction and provision if he was supposed to take this leap of faith.

God not only told Nehemiah exactly what he needed, He also provided the perfect opportunity for Nehemiah to make these requests known to someone with all the power necessary to bring them to fruition. And even though there was still plenty of unknown, Nehemiah walked in obedience. This is an example of faith being louder than fear!

In your life today, God will send people to act on His behalf to provide for and support His plan for you. All you have to do is be ready to ask and open to obey. If you don't have what you need yet, you're not ready yet. If you don't know the next steps, *pray*. If you want to know how to request what you need, *pray*. If you need courage to take the next step, *pray*. Ask Him where He's leading you and what you need to walk in it well.

Heavenly Father, thank You for having all the answers even when I don't. Remind me to come before You in prayer with my questions and fears instead of spiraling and stressing about figuring it out myself. I want to have a bold faith that's not afraid to ask for what I need. In Jesus' name, amen.

39

It's Not a Punishment, It's a Preparation

King Darius wrote... "Peace be multiplied to you. I make a decree, that in all my royal dominion people are to tremble and fear before the God of Daniel."

Daniel 6:25-26

When my company told me I couldn't work there while also running the Abundantly More Community, I was devastated. A million anxious thoughts ran through my head. *How could this be happening? God, I did everything You asked me to do. You promised You'd provide abundantly. Why is this plan falling apart?* With tears streaming down my face and heart racing, I called my dad. As I sobbed and explained what had happened, he listened quietly and then responded, "Do you believe God called you to take this step of faith?" Without hesitation, I answered, "Yes!" Then he said, "Well, why don't you just act as though you have a million dollars in the bank, and let Him do the rest?" *How could Dad say that?* He noticed my hesitation and gently but firmly answered, "I know it's scary, but do you trust God?"

Often God has us exactly where He wants us, ready to deliver us in a way that's too abundant for us to take credit for. The problem is we can block our own blessings by letting our faith be dictated by our circumstances rather than our Creator.

Do you ever say you want a miracle, but you don't want to be in the position to need one if it's uncomfortable? You say you want God's plan for your life, but you get discouraged when life isn't going the way *you* planned? Or you want to be used for His glory, but you don't want to be in a situation where you need to depend on Him?

We've all been there. Remember, God didn't prepare Daniel for the lions' den by teaching him how to tame lions; He prepared him in the prayer closet. The way the Lord prepares you is far more powerful than any worldly experience could ever be. As my dad always says, "God leads us through different circumstances to ask us the same question: 'Do you trust Me?'" His kindness will lead you through situations where your faith will grow. When you are outside your comfort zone, only then can you experience what's possible through faith.

When Daniel was thrown into the lions' den, that didn't mean he had failed. In fact, it was because of his faith that the Lord used him to display His glory. Seek His purpose for you in this season and cling even more tightly to His promises. He hasn't abandoned you. He's preparing to use you.

Heavenly Father, thank You for using even my most devastating circumstances for Your good. Help me to walk by faith when my fear is crippling. Please reveal how You want to work in and through me in this season, and give me confidence to trust in Your provision even when it feels like I'm walking into a lions' den. In Jesus' name, amen.

GOD IS PREPARING TO USE YOU

40

Your Brokenness Is Not Your Identity

But we have this treasure in jars of clay, to show that the surpassing power belongs to God and not to us. We are afflicted in every way, but not crushed; perplexed, but not driven to despair; persecuted, but not forsaken; struck down, but not destroyed.

2 Corinthians 4:7–9

When I told my parents I was pregnant, I was in the middle of a divorce with my child's father. My pregnancy announcement came as a complete shock to *most* of the people around me. Soon I was flooded with messages like "How did you not know?" and "Do you know who the father is?" It wasn't what little girls think of when dreaming about becoming a mother. In fact, I found myself rushing to explain my "situation" to anyone who would listen, trying to correct any assumptions they might have seeing my pregnant belly and no ring on my finger. Even after my son was born, I felt so much shame around being a single mom. And I felt alone in this shame.

Because the Lord created us for community, the Enemy loves to isolate us so that we feel alone. Thankfully, the Lord both convicted and comforted me, saying, "How you got here isn't what matters. What matters is what I'll do from here." Sister, once I surrendered my narrative to the Lord, that *changed everything*. I was able to share my struggle in community. I discovered I wasn't alone at all. My identity wasn't in my brokenness.

Can you think of a time when someone shared an honest take on a tough time in their life, not knowing you were walking through the same thing? I'll bet it made you feel less alone. Maybe they pulled back the curtain on marriage struggles. Or infertility. Or financial hardship. The lie Satan wants us to believe is that if others find out what's really going on, it would change the way they view us. But God dispels that lie.

Your *wrestle* doesn't disqualify you, and your struggle doesn't mean you've failed. Paul reminded us that although we're pressed on every side by troubles, we're not crushed. We may be perplexed, but not driven to despair. We may be persecuted, but never abandoned by God. We may be knocked down, but not destroyed.

Graciously, God allowed me to see how my difficult season would be used to bless others. But sometimes you won't see the full picture for why you're struggling. In fact, you might not see it until you get to heaven. But I promise you, what He's doing right now in this very season is a crucial part to an incredible plan. Trust Him.

Heavenly Father, thank You for using my brokenness to shine Your light. Help me to find my identity in You, not in my brokenness. Lord, open my eyes to see who I can encourage with what You've taught me in this season, so I can share this hope You've given me. In Jesus' name, amen.

41

He Will Deliver You with What You Already Have

"For to everyone who has will more be given, and he will have an abundance. But from the one who has not, even what he has will be taken away."

Matthew 25:29

My friend Court is the graphic designer for a prominent women's ministry, Live Original. She's an incredibly gifted creative, but what's funny is that when she was offered that job, she didn't have any professional graphic design experience *at all*. You might be thinking, *What? That doesn't make any sense. How did she get such an amazing job with no experience?* And to that, she would respond, "God will always do the opposite of what makes sense to the world!" God saw that the desire of her heart was to create, and He placed the opportunity of a lifetime in her lap. He knew that Court would steward the gift He had given her well, because she cared more about being faithful than being flashy. Her story is a constant reminder to me that He doesn't call the qualified—He qualifies the called.

We all have a gift from God. It could be hospitality, leadership, speaking, creating . . . you name it. What's yours? What comes more naturally to you than anything else? What sets your soul on fire? If you don't know what your gift is, begin by serving in small ways to discover what God might kindle and ignite in you.

When we steward our gift, serving others with it and giving God the glory, He prunes us to remove anything hindering us, allowing us to be even more fruitful. Court had to surrender her desire to be comfortable and to look like she "had it all together." She had to leave her cushy job to walk in obedience in helping to launch Live Original. It wasn't always easy, and at times she felt crazy, but through her sacrifice, boldness, and faithfulness, millions of women have been reached and so many lives have been transformed for Christ. How encouraging, right?!

When you hide your gift, acting as though you're not important or prepared enough to use it, you're missing the opportunities God has for you to impact others and display His love through it. As a result, He has to give that mission to someone else who *will* answer the call.

Resist any temptation to say no to the Lord, passing on something you feel too good for, or waiting for Him to bring you something bigger. And don't throw away what He's already given you, even if it feels like a burden or the weight is too much to bear. Ask Him how to navigate the journey He has you on, and He will show you the way. He wants to work *in* you before He works *through* you.

Heavenly Father, thank You for the gifts You're entrusted me with. On days where I struggle to see my purpose, help me rest in my identity and worthiness as Your child. Equip me with the boldness I need to pursue the calling You've placed on my life, so I can point others to You. In Jesus' name, amen.

42

Pour Out and You Will Not Run Empty

If you pour yourself out for the hungry and satisfy the desire of the afflicted, then shall your light rise in the darkness and your gloom be as the noonday. And the LORD will guide you continually and satisfy your desire in scorched places and make your bones strong; and you shall be like a watered garden, like a spring of water, whose waters do not fail.

Isaiah 58:10-11

One time when I was invited to a worship night, the Lord made it clear He wanted me there. But as the day arrived, I wasn't so sure. I was going with a totally new group of friends, I had my baby with me, and it was on a Sunday night after a long day of serving at church. Everything in me wanted to go home, but something in my spirit whispered that if my flesh wanted to stay away that badly, there might be an opportunity to be a blessing there. So I prayed that God would give me supernatural strength.

Within fifteen minutes of being there, I met her. I don't even remember the young woman's name now, but she poured her heart out to me about what she was walking through in that season, feeling alone and confused. And I was able to encourage her with exactly what the Lord had been teaching me. I left that night feeling energized, refreshed, and restored.

How often do you feel too tired to pour out? Maybe Sundays are your only days off, so you don't want to use them to serve at church. Maybe you have such a busy schedule that hosting a Bible study or connecting intentionally with a friend isn't convenient. Maybe when someone reaches out to you for advice, you're so focused on your own problems that you have no capacity to help them.

Pouring yourself out for the needs of others not only allows the Lord to refresh and restore you, but also to rebuild you. When you're running on empty, it's easier to hold on to something that might actually be draining your capacity to do what He's called you to—whether that's anger, bitterness, resentment, unforgiveness, or unworthiness. Sister, it's time to ask the Lord what you need to break off and rebuke what's holding you back from receiving the fullness He has for you. Don't let pride or fatigue get in the way of how the Lord wants to fill you.

Heavenly Father, thank You for pouring back into me when I am feeling empty. Help me to pour out freely, with faith that You will replenish me better than I could imagine. I want to receive everything You have for me, and I don't want to hold on to what You've called me to bless others with. In Jesus' name, amen.

43
You're Not Failing, You're Being Tested

Blessed is the man who remains steadfast under trial, for when he has stood the test he will receive the crown of life, which God has promised to those who love him.

James 1:12

For a long time, I thought that if I were a "good enough" Christian, the Lord would reward my hard work, and life would go according to plan. So understandably, I was discouraged when, rather than seeing my hard work result in steps forward, I was taking steps back. I had many conversations with the Lord, asking, "What gives? I know You've called me to this, but instead of success, I'm seeing failure. What am I doing wrong?" I believe the reason I wasn't seeing progress wasn't because I was doing something wrong, but because my faith was being tested so He could lead me to what He had for me.

It could be that you're not failing, sister, you're being tested. And you're being tested because you've proven yourself worthy of the call. Celebrate the fact that God is not leaving you where you're comfortable but leading you into something so much bigger than you. It requires pruning, it requires discipline, and it requires faith—more faith than your desire to avoid hardship—to access the fullness God has for you.

The trial you're walking through isn't a punishment or a result of your failure. Even though you can't see it now, it's God's kindness to remove from you what is no longer serving you, even if it's keeping you comfortable. The heart of God is not to control you. It's not to take away what or who you love. The heart of God is for you to be filled, sustained, and secure only in what can never be taken from you, which is Him.

You can expect the trials, so don't be caught off guard by them. Prepare for them accordingly. When you're tempted to run, *remain*. This test is a part of your testimony, and it will equip you for impact and purpose beyond your wildest dreams.

The most discouraging part about the testing can be the lies from the Enemy that tempt us to believe our trials are somehow our fault. These lies cause us to question God's faithfulness and provision, even though He's promised that these trials are to prosper us and not to harm us (Jeremiah 29:11). Our God is a God who keeps His promises. There is honor and reward waiting for you. And rest assured, the trials you're walking through in this season are not for nothing.

Heavenly Father, help me shift my perspective when I'm walking through trials, seeing them as preparation for Your plan rather than as punishment. Thank You for the hope I can cling to when I'm tempted to give up, and the confidence to know that it's for a purpose bigger than I can imagine. In Jesus' name, amen.

44

God Can Change Your Reality in an Instant

As Saul turned to leave Samuel, God changed Saul's heart, and all these signs were fulfilled that day.

1 Samuel 10:9 NIV

It's really hard for me to ask for help. Have I mentioned that already? Because it really is!

Usually, I wait to reach out until I'm completely burnt out, there's absolutely no possible way I can do it on my own, and my only chance of survival is asking someone else for support. The Lord has shown me so many times that often the reason He allows us to be in a place of need is for others to answer His call and be a part of the blessing.

I remember like it was yesterday, reaching a point of burnout and feeling so defeated that I couldn't manage my entire community on my own. I was determined to do everything myself, and I was totally failing. The Lord kept nudging me to reach out and ask for help, and I refused. Finally, I was writing a devotion in which I said, "We weren't meant to do life alone," and the Holy Spirit opened my eyes to realize that I wasn't supposed to do *this* alone, either!

So I reached out to a friend, and she immediately responded, "Oh my gosh! This is *exactly* what I've been praying for!" Wow. God always has our best interest at heart.

Your calling and success have nothing to do with your qualifications and everything to do with your obedience. When you're faithful with the small things, that's when you get blessed with the big things.

His timing isn't always something you can make sense of or predict. God moves when your heart is in the right posture to steward His next step well. So live as though your prayers will be answered and His plan will be brought to fruition tomorrow. How could you make the most of today? Could you bake cookies for a neighbor, apologize to a friend, forgive a family member, write a letter to someone you love, celebrate someone you've been too busy to reach out to?

If all your prayers were answered tomorrow, would you be ready to receive them? Do you have the budget for the finances you're praying for, the friends to host in the house you've been asking for, the business plan for the work changes you want, the healing you need for the relationship you've been desiring? God's been ready for your next step. Are you? He moves when *you* are ready.

He can change your reality in an instant.

Heavenly Father, I know You are capable of miracles and rejoice to perform them for those who have faith to see them come to fruition. Help me believe that You will more in my life in ways that can only be identified as miracles. I want other people to see You work in and through me and be led to You as a result. In Jesus' name, amen.

45
Be Faithful with Little

"Whoever can be trusted with very little can also be trusted with much, and whoever is dishonest with very little will also be dishonest with much."

Luke 16:10 NIV

For so long, I found myself bitter and angry with God for my struggle with finances. It felt like one thing after another would fall through the cracks, and I was barely scraping by each month. I begged God to just drop a big fat check in my lap so that I could finally breathe. I even asked for it in faith! I remember praying, "Lord, if you just give me $10,000, I'll be set." I heard Him respond, *What would you do with it?* I immediately thought of how I would spend it. I could catch up on rent, pay off debt, add to my savings, and not worry about putting food on the table for Harv. But as soon as I thought these thoughts, I was taken aback. God convicted me.

He showed me that He cares so much more about what I do with what I already have, how I steward what He has given me, than what I don't have. If I could be faithful with the little I had, I could also be faithful with more. That's not to say I was foolishly spending money, or that I would perfectly manage more money now. But it was a reminder that God cares about what we have—whatever that amount is, and whether it's money or some other resource.

Maybe your battle right now isn't over finances, but you've found yourself angry with God over something that's missing or lacking. God is not your enemy here. Satan wants you to spend all your energy attacking anything except himself, the actual Enemy. He wants you so focused on who or what you think is responsible for your current circumstances that you forget about the One who has the power to change them. Your *real* Enemy is working hard behind the scenes to get you so wound up, you can't even see the doors the Lord is opening to deliver you through.

Maybe you're feeling discouraged, convinced that the reason for your struggle is your finances, your spouse (or lack of one), your friend, that family member, or whatever else you're blaming for what is or isn't happening in your life. But nothing, and no one, is powerful enough to take from you what God has for you.

The Lord will use every single step in your journey to equip you with exactly what you need for what's next. Even the seasons that feel hopeless have purpose, but you must draw near to God to discover what He wants to do in and through you here.

Heavenly Father, thank You for using even the most difficult seasons for my good. Help me to seek You and draw near to You when my pain and disappointment feel too heavy to carry on my own. Give me eyes to see Your Truth when it's so tempting to believe the Enemy's lies. I know You have an abundant plan for my life. In Jesus' name, amen.

46

"Do I Not Send You?"

And Gideon said to him, "Please, my lord, if the LORD is with us, why then has all this happened to us? And where are all his wonderful deeds that our fathers recounted to us, saying, 'Did not the LORD bring us up from Egypt?' But now the LORD has forsaken us and given us into the hand of Midian." And the LORD turned to him and said, "Go in this might of yours and save Israel from the hand of Midian; do not I send you?"

Judges 6:13–14

"Why me, God?" I asked as I sobbed uncontrollably. "I'm tired. So, so tired. I can't do this. I just can't do this." After a particularly rough week with Harv not sleeping, an unexpected bill draining my almost-negative bank account, and depression threatening to take over, I felt like giving up.

I was defeated, overwhelmed, and every glimmer of hope I once had was gone. I waited, sat, prayed, and had nearly fallen asleep holding Harv when I heard God whisper, *You* can't *do this . . . without Me*. I wanted to say, "Well, it doesn't look like I'm doing it *with* You, either. Have You even been paying attention?" As I journaled through my fears and frustration, and this response from the Lord, He began revealing to me that I was still attempting things in my own strength that were only placed in my lap to be accomplished through His strength.

It's so easy to get caught up in the "why?" when life isn't going our way. "Why is this happening to me?" "Does God even see me?" "Does He care?"

Like Gideon in today's scripture, maybe you've seen and heard God do mighty things, but now you are questioning if He is who He says He is because you're not seeing those mighty things happen for you. If so, this isn't happening to *destroy* you; it's happening to *develop* you.

Maybe you're afraid to move forward, thinking you don't have what it takes to defeat the Enemy, but in reality, you've already been given everything you need. You're not a victim in this battle; you're the *victor*. So if you're feeling defenseless, call upon your Defender and ask Him to equip you for what's ahead.

When you feel as though you're being "forced out" from where you once felt so comfortable, that's the Lord nudging you forward, saying, "I love you too much to leave you here." He's calling you to *go*. His response to the victory you're looking for is, "Did I not send you?"

Heavenly Father, forgive me for getting so worked up about my situation, assuming You had forgotten about me when really You were preparing a way for me that I just couldn't see because it didn't look like my own plan. Thank You for calling me to things so much bigger than I thought I'd be capable of. In Jesus' name, amen.

HE'S NOT DONE WITH YOU YET

47
Run Your Race with Endurance

Therefore, since we are surrounded by so great a cloud of witnesses, let us also lay aside every weight, and sin which clings so closely, and let us run with endurance the race that is set before us, looking to Jesus, the founder and perfecter of our faith, who for the joy that was set before him endured the cross, despising the shame, and is seated at the right hand of the throne of God.

Hebrews 12:1-2

As Harv and I started a brand-new adventure in our first place together, our cute little trailer, I was so scared. It would be my first time living by myself as a mom, and I was dreading the cold, hard reality of being alone. My only hope was to fix my eyes on Jesus, trusting that He was preparing a plan for me even better than one I could plan for myself.

When you're tempted to believe the lie that you're alone, open the Word. You're surrounded by witnesses who have experienced the faithfulness of God. You're not called to run this race alone; you're called to receive the baton and pass it forward. Sin clings and weight bears down. You must continuously cast off what is not from Christ if you want to run with endurance.

Have you ever looked to the side when you're driving, only to notice that you started veering off in that same direction? Where you're looking determines the direction you'll go. If you are looking left and right, you'll get distracted. If you're looking down, you'll fall. If you look to God, the stumbling blocks the Enemy tries to throw at you won't get you off course. You can only stumble when you take your eyes off Jesus.

Do not allow the Enemy to rob you of your joy because you are not yet where you want to be in life. You have the ability to multiply what the Lord has given you if you steward it well and are obedient to Him. The race He's called you to is not a sprint—it's a marathon—and the course has been thoughtfully laid out before you. You may be weary, but you're not done.

Your reward for enduring the race is a close relationship with Christ here on earth and eternity with Him in heaven. Don't let what you do or do not have determine your joy. Your joy is from a source that will never run dry and is an overflow of your surrender to the Holy Spirit, not your circumstances.

Heavenly Father, thank You for enduring the cross so that I could receive salvation. Help me to see the opportunities to be an image bearer through my suffering and point others to You. Forgive me for focusing more on my problems than Your purpose. I want to walk in faith and pass the baton as those before me have done. In Jesus' name, amen.

48

Being Busy Is Not the Same as Being Fruitful

Martha was distracted with much serving. And she went up to him and said, "Lord, do you not care that my sister has left me to serve alone? Tell her then to help me." But the Lord answered her, "Martha, Martha, you are anxious and troubled about many things, but one thing is necessary. Mary has chosen the good portion, which will not be taken away from her."

Luke 10:40–42

There was an entire year when every time someone asked me how I was doing, I responded, "I have so much to do." No joke. People even began to ask and then interrupt, saying, "Let me guess—you have so much to do?" I wore busyness as a badge. Just the thought of being busy was keeping me busy! And because being busy was so overwhelming, I really wasn't accomplishing much at all.

Being busy is not the same thing as being fruitful. God doesn't need you to be busy to make an impact; He needs you to be obedient. Busyness causes us to miss the whispers of God's direction. God doesn't need "progress" and "productivity" to do miracles. He needs faith. He needs surrender.

The story of Mary and Martha is a great example of this. Martha had noble intentions by inviting Jesus into her home, but then she was distracted by her own priorities, blinded to the power of His presence. She even went as far as to ask Him, "Do You not care?" when she was busy with her tasks—while Mary sat at Jesus' feet. How many of us ask Jesus, "Do You not care?" We assume He's neglecting us when He's actually trying to teach us.

If you're an overachiever like me, I know it can be infuriating to think that all your hard work is pointless. It's valid to want your effort recognized, but you don't get brownie points by bearing a burden you were never called to.

When I look at Martha, I feel like I'm staring into a mirror. She wanted Jesus to affirm her in what she was doing *when it was actually the last thing He wanted her to be doing*. How often do we get frustrated if what we're doing isn't acknowledged or supported? How often do we think that God doesn't care about the work we do, that He wants us to trade our busyness for His presence? His presence is enough. His Word is enough. There's nothing wrong with doing, but first we must *dwell*.

Heavenly Father, thank You for the gift of Your presence and for making it so freely available. Help me learn to slow down, release my to-do list, and rest in You. I don't want to be distracted by my own priorities. I want to dwell with You in Your courts. In Jesus' name, amen.

49
"I Am Doing a New Thing"

"Remember not the former things, nor consider the things of old. Behold, I am doing a new thing; now it springs forth, do you not perceive it? I will make a way in the wilderness and rivers in the desert."

Isaiah 43:18-19

My friend Chandler is more determined than anyone I know. During the time I've known her, she's hustled hard to bring the dreams that God has put on her heart to life, and she's walked through some pretty painful things in the process. Most recently, she had a job that was terribly toxic and incredibly draining. She hesitated to leave, because she didn't want to lose the financial security for her family. The job became increasingly untenable as the workload overflowed into family time, and there were growing signs she should quit. But she thought, *I can stick it out for a few more months. I've got to . . .* She had grown so comfortable in the chaos, she didn't even realize how it was affecting her.

Suddenly, God shut the door for Chandler at her job, making it clear it wasn't what He had for her. It's no surprise that, as soon as she left that job, she learned she was pregnant, and the Lord began to stir her desire to start a business to support women walking through infertility and pregnancy after loss—a journey she knew well. He led her out of her comfort so she could walk into her calling.

If God can make a way in the wilderness and rivers in the desert, He can make you a new creation and use your life to have a bigger impact than you ever dreamed. Don't doubt God or rule out what He wants to do based on what you think is realistic. He's planning to do something miraculous. But if your mind is fixated in the present, or stuck in the past, you won't be able to see what God's preparing you for in the future.

The voice of the Lord calls you forward; it's the voice of the Enemy that pulls you back. So if God's calling you into something or forcing you out of something, before you run, retreat, or isolate, ask yourself, *Could God be doing a new thing?* Don't confuse your own fear or anxiety for lack of confirmation or direction from the Lord. He makes it clear, not easy.

Heavenly Father, thank You for the forgiveness of my past mistakes and the future You're planning for me that I do not deserve. Help me cling tightly to Your promises and believe for the impossible. I trust that You are in control and doing something bigger than my mind can comprehend. Thank You for being such a good Father. In Jesus' name, amen.

50
Confident in Christ

For by grace you have been saved through faith.
And this is not your own doing; it is the gift of God,
not a result of works, so that no one may boast.

Ephesians 2:8-9

Right before my friend Enaka and I moved out of the apartment we shared, God sent someone to offer me a job that would relocate me. Only problem? The official offer would come about a week before our lease ended. I was terrified but prayed for confirmation. I kept seeing stories of Noah and his obedience to do something that wouldn't make any sense at all—until its purpose was revealed. Trusting God, I sold everything I had, packed up only what I needed, and waited.

As that move-out date neared, I learned that the job offer wouldn't be for another few weeks. *What?* I was gutted. My community surrounded me with support, and I moved into a friend's spare bedroom. But the weeks turned to months, and finally I had to make the devastating decision to walk away from that job. Shortly afterward, a friend offered the perfect living space for Harv and me. It was in my budget and close by the friends I loved so dearly. Suddenly, all the difficulty we had endured made sense.

Do you ever notice how the Lord brings you through a valley before taking you to the mountaintops? It's because we tend to draw nearest to Him when we recognize our need for Him. Maybe a job opportunity fell through, your finances are tight, you have too much on your plate, or something else has pushed you completely out of your comfort zone. I truly believe that's His kindness, to allow us to fully grasp how out of control our own lives are, because when we surrender our plans to Him, He guides us.

The Bible says that God's plan for you is better than you can imagine—and that it won't be accomplished in your own strength. If I'm honest, I really wrestle with this. I love walking into situations where I'm totally confident that I'm prepared. But walking into situations where my confidence is in Christ, and Christ alone? That takes a lot more work for me.

Walking by faith always comes with a risk that your plan might fail, but your plan failing just means His is coming to fruition. Put your faith in Him today.

Heavenly Father, thank You for the gift of salvation, and for creating an abundant future for me that's not dependent on my own strength or ability. Please increase my faith in Your plan, Lord. I want to live expectantly for miracles and be used as a vessel for Your glory. In Jesus' name, amen.

51

Delight in the Lord, and
He Will Uphold You

The steps of a man are established by the LORD, when he delights in his way; though he fall, he shall not be cast headlong, for the LORD upholds his hand.

Psalm 37:23-24

Before Harv was born, I had built a platform on social media and was making sales through affiliate links and influencing. I was filming and posting consistently throughout my day, going live, and sharing "in real time" moments and thoughts constantly. But as a new mom, that pace felt impossible to maintain. I was coaching others on how to run their own social media, offering virtual assistance and content creation services, helping them sign brand deals—but I wasn't getting those deals myself. I was willing to do *anything* to earn an income, but it felt like God was shutting the door on every opportunity for me.

One day the Lord told me to humble myself and share my story with others so that they might be encouraged. As you may know, I said yes. Because that video went viral, it led to opportunities and provision like I never dreamed. I had just needed to obey God.

The Lord has established a plan for your life. Period. Do you want it? You can choose to walk in faith in His plan, obeying the things He calls you to and trusting His outcome. Or you can choose to live in doubt and do what feels or sounds best to you in the moment. You can't do both. You can only see as far as the near future, but He can see as far as eternity. Whose plan will you follow?

Psalm 37 says, "The steps of a man are established by the LORD, when he delights in his way" (v. 23). Do you delight in the Lord and His way? Is He your joy? You won't find joy or security in your success, opportunities, financial stability, or anything else. You'll only know true delight in the Lord.

And the more we delight in the Lord, the more we delight in obeying Him. If we want the Lord to guide and uphold us, we must be willing to lay down our pride, drop the illusion that we have it all together, and pivot toward what He's calling us to. Pivoting has nothing to do with failure and everything to do with faith.

Verse 24 says you will not be cast out if you delight in the Lord. It may feel like it, but you can rebuke that lie and trust that the refinement or trial represents pruning, which the Lord does only to those who are fruitful. You're right where you're supposed to be, friend.

Heavenly Father, thank You for establishing my steps. I so want to honor You and be trusted with a higher calling that I tend to strive or hustle for what I think You want or expect me to do. Help me learn to slow down, seek You in the chaos, and discern Your voice telling me what to do and where to go. I want to delight in You and only You. In Jesus' name, amen.

52
Hope Isn't Found in What's Seen

So we do not lose heart. Though our outer self is wasting away, our inner self is being renewed day by day. For this light momentary affliction is preparing for us an eternal weight of glory beyond all comparison, as we look not to the things that are seen but to the things that are unseen. For the things that are seen are transient, but the things that are unseen are eternal.

2 Corinthians 4:16–18

A while back, I felt like I was failing God and failing my son—*over and over*. My best friend and I saw an opportunity to sign with a popular podcast network, but in the end, we fell short of the network's requirements. Within two weeks, three of the tires on my new car— that I could barely afford—shredded as I was driving. A few weeks later, my car refused to start at all! My mental health was suffering. I felt like God had given me the open doors I'd prayed for, but I was dropping the ball and totally disappointing Him.

As I sat in my tiny mobile home, praying for help, my son's dad, David, reached out and offered to fly us to his home so we could have some support. What I saw as being little more than a kind gesture ended up being the very trip God would use to bring us back together and reconcile our family.

You may feel discouraged today because you think you've disappointed God. Maybe you feel so far from where you want to be that you're wondering if it's even worth pressing on. You know deep down that you were made for more, but you're struggling to remember His promises in the midst of your own problems. Sister, I get it.

After weeks of being on my knees, asking God to change my circumstances, He spoke to me so clearly, saying, *I need you to meet the end of yourself, if you want what I have for you.* Just a few months later I was walking in answered prayers that once felt impossible.

The Lord doesn't need success to advance us. He needs surrender.

Sister, on this side of heaven you may never fully know the purpose for the trials in this season. But you can be confident that seeking Christ *in it* and exemplifying Him *through it* will reap a bountiful harvest if you do not give up.

Heavenly Father, thank You for creating me for a purpose and a plan bigger than I can see right now. In the midst of my struggles, please cover me with Your peace and strength and remind me that my hope does not rest in what is seen, but in what is unseen. In Jesus' name, amen.

You Were Made For More

53

Your Weakness Is a Vessel for His Glory

But he said to me, "My grace is sufficient for you, for my power is made perfect in weakness." Therefore I will boast all the more gladly of my weaknesses, so that the power of Christ may rest upon me.

2 Corinthians 12:9

As a type-A overachiever and people pleaser, I experience burnout and overwhelm more often than I'd like to admit. The dishes need to be done, groceries need to be bought, money needs to be made to buy the groceries, the laundry needs to be run, I'm exhausted because I was up all night with a baby who didn't sleep, I forgot to call back my friend, and I woke up in a panic because I'd forgotten to pay a bill.

I'm afraid to say no, so I heap higher expectations on myself than anyone else ever would. There have been many, many moments when I've felt crippled by the length of my to-do list and how far behind I feel.

What about you? Feeling tired, burnt out, or overwhelmed is not a reflection of you not being "good enough." It's a gentle nudge from the Lord to give the burdens you're carrying to Him. He'll lead you to where you will recognize your need for Him, because only then can you receive the fullness He has for you.

If you're anything like me, instead of seeing your shortcomings as an invitation to surrender, you wrestle with feeling like you need to do *more*. Work harder. Hustle. Strive. It's a cycle that repeats itself.

Do you ever get caught in this cycle? Friend, you're not alone, and I want to encourage you. An area where you're in need is usually an indicator that the Lord wants to do something bigger. He wants to strengthen you, redirect you, or draw you closer to Him. And to do this, He allows something that once flowed smoothly—health, finances, relationships, parenting, work—to slowly lose momentum. He'll use these things so that you'll seek Him much more intently when you realize how desperately you need Him.

There's no way you can handle what God is calling you to, outside of Him. So stop believing the lie that you're not enough just because you have no idea how to navigate what's ahead! No matter how daunting or difficult your situation seems, it's an assignment. And that means He's prepared to equip you. Each time, He'll ask the same question in a different way: *Do you trust Me?*

Heavenly Father, thank You for reminding me that my value and purpose do not depend on my success or accomplishments. Help me to see my weakness as an opportunity to surrender my burdens to You rather than be ashamed of them. Give me eyes to see what I need to lay down at Your feet. In Jesus' name, amen.

54
Faith in Your Defender

And Haman said to the king, "For the man whom the king delights to honor, let royal robes be brought, which the king has worn, and the horse that the king has ridden, and on whose head a royal crown is set." . . . Then the king said to Haman, "Hurry; take the robes and the horse, as you have said, and do so to Mordecai the Jew. . . . Leave out nothing that you have mentioned."

Esther 6:7–8, 10

There was an extended family member who I believed was my opponent for quite some time. It seemed like everywhere I went, I was told that they had gone before me to get or give information to paint me in a bad light. I felt so defeated. One day I was venting about how frustrated I felt, and my dad said, "Have you tried praying for them? I'm sure there's something God wants to do in their heart through this too." As annoyed as I was that he would suggest that—instead of joining me in my pity party—I agreed. Soon this person was reaching out, asking how they could help me. I'll never forget how God used even a perceived enemy to refine me and set me up for a blessing.

If you feel weighed down or defeated by your adversaries today, I want to encourage you with a story of Queen Esther's uncle, Mordecai.

The king's right-hand man, Haman, hated Mordecai. Mordecai was incredibly vocal about his faith and loyalty to God, which threatened Haman's ego. So much so, he developed a plan to bring before the king in an attempt to have Mordecai put to death. The night before Haman intended to present this plan, the king lay in bed awake. Because he couldn't sleep, he asked his servants to read to him from a book of people who had done good deeds. Mordecai was one of those people, and the king immediately asked if Mordecai had ever been recognized for his kindness. The next day the king asked how he should honor someone who deserved the highest praise. Haman, pridefully assuming the king planned to honor him, gave him elaborate ideas, not sparing any expense. Then the king instructed Haman to arrange for all these things to be prepared for . . . *Mordecai*.

God is always at work behind the scenes in ways you could never orchestrate yourself. Mordecai trusted God's plan and walked in confidence, expectant of a victory. Can I encourage you to walk with this same level of confidence in Christ today, and watch how your faith changes your circumstances?

Heavenly Father, thank You for fighting on my behalf and orchestrating opportunities and provision I could never make happen on my own. Help me to remember that You are so much more powerful than my opponent, and my future is in Your hands. Give me courage to walk by faith into the plans You have for me. In Jesus' name, amen.

55

No One Is More Equipped for Your Call Than You

As for you, always be sober-minded, endure suffering, do the work of an evangelist, fulfill your ministry.

2 Timothy 4:5

I'll never forget when I heard the Lord tell me to share my story of single motherhood on social media. I was absolutely terrified, and for weeks I found every reason not to. But no matter how much I tried to resist, God kept putting it on my heart, which is how I knew that, no matter how scary it felt, I needed to do it. I thought in that act of obedience He was just going to teach me a lesson in humility and encourage some people along the way. I had no idea He would use it to change my life.

Can you relate? Is something holding you back from stepping out in faith? The resistance you feel about moving forward is no surprise, because when you're walking in your calling, you're also creating space for someone else to walk in theirs. Maybe the lie you've believed is that if you're not *totally* prepared, you shouldn't move at all—but that couldn't be further from the truth. The Enemy is shaking in his boots at the thought of you moving, because when you step out in faith, you activate the body of Christ. If you take action,

God will empower others to come together, forming a bigger impact than you could have ever had on your own.

Maybe you're thinking, *Girl, I have no* idea *what my ministry is!* If so, let me ask you a question: What's something that God has put on your heart that keeps getting shoved to the back burner? Maybe you feel like it's not the right timing or you're not ready yet, or maybe you *want* to take action, but every time you try, the chaos of life gets in the way. It might be a business venture, a ministry, a Bible study you want to start, a book you want to write, a habit you want to form (or break), or something you want to create that stays lodged in the back of your mind—no matter how hard you try to shake it free. That could be the thing God has for you to pursue now.

Make no mistake: God has uniquely equipped you with the gifts, skills, and passions you need to carry out His abundant plan for you. Any doubt, fear, or insecurity you feel is simply the Enemy trying to keep you from experiencing it. Can I encourage you to rebuke those lies today? No one is more qualified for your calling than you.

Heavenly Father, thank You for creating me with unique gifts and passions. I rebuke the lie that I'm not enough, and I surrender my desire to race ahead rather than steward what's right in front of me. I receive the fullness You have for me and the refinement required to carry it well. In Jesus' name, amen.

56
This Is Our Confidence

And this is the confidence that we have toward him, that
if we ask anything according to his will he hears us.

1 John 5:14

At a time when I really needed provision, I had applied for Harv and
me to live in a low-income housing development. My hopes were
high, but my application was rejected. I cried out to God, asking
why He'd left me hanging. *Where are you, God? Can't you see we need
You?* I was starting to think that God wasn't even listening. But that
wasn't true at all.

Within a few weeks, a friend reached out about having a mobile
home for rent that was the perfect size for us. And—as I shared
earlier—although I'd sold most of our belongings, the Lord sent
strangers to gift us, out of the kindness of their hearts, exactly what
we needed.

God blessed me, and I don't mean just with material provisions.
He gave me the comfort of the Holy Spirit, a community of fellow
believers, and most importantly, the confidence that no matter what,
He heard me.

God hears you too. That doesn't mean you'll get exactly what you
want, because He brings the desires of your heart to fruition when
it's according to His will. I know it's easy to feel discouraged—to
believe the lie that He doesn't see you, doesn't hear you, or just

doesn't care when you're crying out to Him and your circumstances aren't changing. But He's there. Give Him everything that's weighing on you and *trust* that He is at work.

Even when it seems that God is silent, because He's not changing your situation, rest assured He's changing you through it. There's nothing and no one powerful enough to take away what God has for you. If you want to see Him move, ask Him what He needs to build in or break off you so that you can be used for miracles beyond your own capacity.

That's right: the Lord wants to use you as a willing vessel to build His kingdom and bless others in Jesus' name. So stop waiting until you hit rock bottom to intercede for what you need. Don't be afraid of a "no" or "not yet." (You might get 'em!) Ask with boldness and then walk as though your struggle has already been taken care of. Come into agreement with His desire to work through you, and ask Him for what you need to pour out abundantly and bless others.

Heavenly Father, thank You for hearing my prayers. During seasons when I struggle to feel Your presence or hear Your voice, help me to remember that You are there, and that my trials are not in vain. Give me courage to ask for what I need and to trust that You will provide for my every need. In Jesus' name, amen.

57

What Is Your Source?

"I am the true vine, and my Father is the vinedresser."

John 15:1

When I'm anticipating doing something that scares me, or I feel behind, I try to avoid that situation. Before I know it, I've spent hours scrolling on my phone, driving around doing random errands, or manically cleaning the house so I can justify "not having the time" to do that thing, thereby avoiding it. It's a toxic cycle that leads to isolation and failure time and time again, all because I choose to avoid the hard stuff rather than lean into it.

Being connected to the *true* vine brings ease, not anxiety. It brings peace when I would have been striving for perfection. It brings comfort when I would have been looking for ways to control.

What helps you cope? Where do you "plug in" most consistently? What do you seek to reconcile or spend time doing when you feel disconnected? I think it's easy to think of addictions or "sins" that seem worse than what you're entertaining to justify your own actions. But even if what you seek most isn't the *worst* thing for you, don't you want what's best?

For me this looks like scrolling on social media, "productive procrastination" by hyper-focusing on cleaning, organizing, or doing errands that aren't the best use of my time, or even jumping to assist others instead of focusing on what's on my own plate.

God will steer you away from some things you're doing that aren't necessarily sinful. There are many reasons for this. Maybe it's to take you out of your comfort zone to prepare you for something bigger that's coming. Maybe it's to set an example for someone else who's struggling in this area. Or maybe it's just to develop discipline in you.

God is a vinedresser, so you can expect to be pruned. Pruning is for the purpose of cutting off anything that is hindering the cultivation of new growth. He'll prune you by leading you through something, calling you out of something, or straight up removing something from your life. Being separated from something we've grown comfortable or familiar with feels painful, right? That is why the Bible often refers to refinement as "dying to your flesh." If we want to become more like Christ, we have to release what satisfies our flesh.

Not every season is a harvest. If you're feeling discouraged by the season you're in right now, I want to remind you how crucial the planting, watering, and pruning are to an abundant harvest. Even a tree that looks dead in the winter bears a bountiful harvest in the spring. This season isn't defining you; it's developing you.

Heavenly Father, thank You for being such a loving Father. Help me to stay rooted in Your grace and receive Your pruning with gratitude for the growth You're preparing me for. It's so hard to simply rest and receive, especially when life isn't going the way that I planned, but I know You have an abundant plan for me. In Jesus' name, amen.

58
Keep Running Your Race

*I have fought the good fight, I have finished
the race, I have kept the faith.*

2 Timothy 4:7

A good friend of mine is in the home stretch of her book being
launched into the world. I've walked this journey with her and have
watched the waves of emotion, energy, and spiritual warfare that
she's experienced in this season. When she's not fueled up with
prayer and rest, she starts to slow down. When she's surrounded
by friends and supporters who are cheering her on, she's sprinting
without even breaking a sweat. Now, with the end in sight, she's fired
up and applying her last bit of energy to finish strong. It's been so
humbling to compare her journey to the personal "spiritual" marathons I feel like I'm running. I've found myself asking, "Am *I* fueled
up so I can finish strong?"

It's easier to start a race than finish it, right? And it's easier to
push to the finish when the adrenaline is pumping. To be honest, a
physical race has never been appealing enough for me to actually
participate in. This does, however, describe my spiritual race!

Once we get going and the excitement wears off, we become
aware of some areas in our bodies that may be weak, or even painful.
We weren't meant to participate in marathons without lots of consistent practice and discipline, because it takes adequate training to

build our muscles to sustain a greater distance than we're used to. We start with shorter distances and work our way up, not rushing it, because building endurance is crucial to finishing the race strong.

We're also not called to run alone, which is why the Enemy tries so hard to disconnect and isolate us. We were made to travel this journey of faith with others. The Enemy wants us to look at the finish line and get discouraged by how far away it seems, not accounting for the miracles the Lord will do. Or the timelines the Lord will collapse along the way. Or the people who will run alongside us.

Faith is a requirement to make it to the finish line, so train your mind to cling to the truth and put aside anything that threatens to take you off course. Your life is not about the outcome, but the journey.

Heavenly Father, thank You for equipping me with the tools I need to run the race You've set before me. When my energy is running low and the finish line feels far, help me to remember that my purpose is walked out in the journey, not in the destination. Increase my faith so I can finish strong, Lord. In Jesus' name, amen.

KEEP RUNNING YOUR RACE

59
The Armor Is Not Optional

Therefore take up the whole armor of God, that
you may be able to withstand in the evil day.

Ephesians 6:13

For the longest time, "putting on the armor of God" was a concept
I was familiar with, but I honestly didn't know exactly how to do it.
Recently, though, I've made a habit of simply praying over and asking
for protection in each area Paul mentioned. I pray that God would
give me eyes to see the truth. That He'd help me pursue righteousness over perfection. That He'd make me a vessel of His supernatural
peace. That He'd increase my faith according to His plan. That He'd
let salvation be my confidence, and that His Spirit would help me
discern any weapon formed against me.

As I go throughout my day and encounter my toddler throwing a
tantrum, being cut off on the highway, or having yet another thing go
wrong, I have to pause in my fleshly response to allow for the armor
of God to kick into gear. It's an active decision at every moment to
pull back the reins on what I want to immediately say or do, and
instead create space for the "weapon" to go to work instead.

In your life, friend, when life is going easy breezy, putting on your
armor might not be your first priority. You feel totally equipped to
handle what's in front of you, because life is good! Right? But no one

walks into battle storing their armor in a backpack. A soldier going to war puts it on ahead of time so they're fully prepared.

Whether you realize it or not, you have an Enemy whose main goal is to keep you from walking in the fullness God has for you. So if Satan is leaving you alone, you're probably laboring all on your own. But chances are, you're reading this book because he's trying to discourage you from moving forward—which means God is preparing you for something the Enemy doesn't want to see come to fruition.

Sister, we must stay vigilant. The command to "take up the full armor" is not a suggestion. If you want to withstand the attacks of the Enemy, your only hope of survival is receiving the resources God has given you. The armor you need is readily available. You don't need a password or a special code to access it. You just need to be insistent and consistent to ask for and put on *all* that you need to be fully effective.

Heavenly Father, help me to make it a habit to put on Your armor every single morning. I want to be fully equipped and prepared for whatever You decide to lead me into, not questioning my own ability because I failed to take up the armor You've given me. Thank You for both fighting my battles and equipping me for them. In Jesus' name, amen.

60

Don't Be Anxious About Tomorrow

"Therefore do not be anxious about tomorrow, for tomorrow will be anxious for itself. Sufficient for the day is its own trouble."

Matthew 6:34

I was sitting in church, feeling particularly discouraged by my finances. They completely consumed my every thought, leaving me feeling anxious and distracted every single day. I remember thinking about money at the very moment my pastor said, "If you could ask God for anything right now, what would it be?" I snapped out of my daze and thought, *Oh my goodness! God must be speaking to me through her to confirm that He hears my requests.*

But what she said next convicted me instead: "When God asked David what he wanted, David responded, 'Just don't take Your Spirit from me.'" *Ouch!* I had been craving an increase in my finances more than I was craving deeper intimacy with the Lord, where all abundance flows from anyway! This started a massive shift in my mindset: a pivot from self-pity when I found myself stressed or anxious, to a posture of worship and praise. It didn't change my circumstances, but it gave me eyes to see what God was doing through them.

If you're in a season where much is out of your control, it may be because the Lord is preparing you to receive what you could not have orchestrated on your own. There's purpose in this season. The way your faith and dependence on God develop now is crucial for what's coming next. Trust Him. Don't be afraid to admit your need or to ask for His help.

You already know the future is getting worked out, so why worry? Tomorrow will be something new that the Lord wants to lead you through or refine you in. What He equips you with today will help you do so, which is why He says not to worry about anything but what's right in front of you.

The Bible says that God's plan for you is better than you can imagine, and it won't be accomplished in your own strength, so you can't boast on it (Ephesians 2:8–9, 3:20). When it's tempting to ask God, "What's next?" or even to beg Him to remove you from your current situation, ask Him instead how He wants to strengthen you through it. God has led you here for a reason.

Heavenly Father, I struggle with surrendering control when life feels chaotic. Help me to remember that I'm not the one in control, whether I feel like it or not. I want to trust You with my whole heart and my whole life. Thank You for never leading me through something I can't handle without You. In Jesus' name, amen.

61
Stewarding Instead of Striving

Many a man proclaims his own steadfast
love, but a faithful man who can find?

Proverbs 20:6

After begging God to bring me a husband, I heard Him clearly ask
me, *If I brought you a husband* right *now, would you be ready?* I looked
around my tiny apartment that was trashed because I was constantly
busy, distracted, trying to accomplish something else. I was suddenly more aware than ever that I could apply that question, "Would
you be ready?" to so many areas of my life. I wanted an increase of
finances, but I wasn't stewarding what I'd been given. I kept saying
that if I just had help with Harv, I'd have more time to do other things,
but I wasn't responsible with the time I did have. I wanted my business to grow, but I wasn't being diligent in the things I knew would
fuel that growth.

If all your prayers were answered tomorrow, *would you be ready?*

Maybe, like me, you've been tempted to believe that your flourishing depends on what you have or don't have. So you feel like the
friends you *don't* have, or what's *not* in your bank account, or the
platform you *don't* have, or the opportunities you *haven't been given*,
or the apology you *haven't* received is what's holding you back from
the life you want. Will you join me in rebuking that lie?

It's a tactic the Enemy has used over and over in my life. And maybe in yours! Satan tries to convince us that if we just had that next thing, we would finally be content—whether it's the car, the home, the job, the friends, the husband, the kids, or the beach house. But it's a trap. None of it will bring you true happiness if you're always chasing the next thing. True joy comes from contentment in Christ.

If you're feeling behind or wanting to rush into what's next, you may be on the verge of experiencing a God-ordained opportunity the Enemy wants to distract you from. *Lean in.* Where you are right now has supernatural purpose, so steward whatever is in front of you today, whether little or much.

Heavenly Father, thank You for all the blessings You've given me that I've taken for granted. Help me to steward the opportunities and relationships You're leading me to in this season with wisdom. I trust that You will provide everything I need in Your perfect timing. In Jesus' name, amen.

62

Keep Your Eyes Fixed on Jesus

If then you have been raised with Christ, seek the
things that are above, where Christ is, seated at
the right hand of God. Set your minds on things
that are above, not on things that are on earth.

Colossians 3:1–2

In the span of just a few weeks I was diagnosed with depression, three tires on my brand-new-to-me car completely shredded (leaving me stranded—yes, three separate times), I fell behind on my rent when I paid for new tires, and everything else went into a tailspin. Oh, *and* my credit card got declined buying nine dollars' worth of food at the store. Here I was, once again at my wits' end, wondering, *Will this season of suffering ever end? I don't know how much more I have to lose.* The anxiety and fear were crippling. I was certain that God had added me to His "strongest soldiers" list without checking my credentials and that I was, in fact, in way over my head.

I remember looking around, counting every reason I had to feel hopeless, and God convicted me, reminding me of every reason I had to be hope*ful.* As I sat worshiping Jesus with my wild, snuggly, smiley baby, a friend knocked on the door with groceries. Then a friend called and needed prayer, and I encouraged her. Then a friend sent a Venmo because I was on her heart. Even without those blessings, my heart was transformed and full of joy, expectant that God would provide in my need.

Maybe you've been through trauma, pain, or hardship, and as a way to protect yourself, you made it your mission to ensure that nothing out of your control *ever* happens again. You plan, organize, clean, dictate, and obsess over details so you know what to expect at all times. The problem? You're not actually in control, and you never will be, especially not if you want God's best for your life. As long as you carry a false sense of control, you'll carry a false sense of peace.

Instead, keep your eyes fixed on Jesus and ask Him to increase your faith. I believe He allows things to happen in your life just to remind you that you're not in control. Not to harm you, but so that you'll seek Him as your source of comfort and security in a world that is full of darkness and disappointment. He wants nothing more than for you to draw close to Him.

Heavenly Father, thank You for the life You saved me from. Help me to keep my eyes fixed on You, and not let what's going on around me distract or discourage me from trusting in Your provision. I know the world doesn't dictate what's possible, because Your plans are bigger than I can even comprehend. Increase my focus and my faith, Lord. In Jesus' name, amen.

HIS PLANS ARE BIGGER THAN YOU KNOW

63
Choose Your Circle Wisely

Whoever walks with the wise becomes wise,
but the companion of fools will suffer harm.

Proverbs 13:20

When I met my business mentor, Erika, for the first time, I was so nervous about trying to impress her. I expected someone who put off an "I'm better than you" attitude. Instead, I encountered one of the most humble, kind, encouraging people I'd ever met. As I got to know her, I realized that being looked up to, respected, and successful had much less to do with what you know, but who you are. Confidence in your identity, ability, and self-worth takes you further and impacts more people than trying to impress them with what you bring to the table.

Erika didn't get to where she was because she was "better"; she was successful because she elevated and empowered others, bringing out the best in them. And she surrounded herself with women who did the same.

I craved those kinds of relationships, and I realized that if I simply shifted my focus from impressing others to impacting them, I would find people who endeavored to do the same. Walking with the wise isn't a "fake it 'til you make it" kind of thing. It's an "align your life with the Word, and you'll find yourself aligned with women who do the same" kind of thing.

So choose who you walk with wisely. With everything you do, you're either growing closer to the Lord or further away. There's no standing still. The people in your life will either convict you or conflict you. Of course there are times they will do both, but which is it most often?

Proverbs 27:17 says that iron sharpens iron; the people you surround yourself with will shape you into who *they* are. Statistically, some say, you're a sum of the five people closest to you. Who are you closest with? The wise or the foolish?

Your circle matters, and sometimes it just takes one person believing in you and breathing life into your vision. One individual can change everything, and you can be the one who changes everything for someone else.

Heavenly Father, I want to grow in wisdom. Help me to connect with women who can come alongside me and walk in the calling You have for us together. I want to be the friend who will encourage others and point them to You, and I want to be surrounded by a community of women who will do the same. In Jesus' name, amen.

64
The Battle Is His

The LORD said to Gideon, "The people with
you are too many for me to give the Midianites
into their hand, lest Israel boast over me,
saying, 'My own hand has saved me.'"

Judges 7:2

When I moved to Nashville as a newly single woman, I truly believed the best was yet to come. I kept saying, "I don't know why I'm here, exactly, I just have a feeling something *big* is going to happen." Well, as you know by now, six weeks later I found out what that something big would be . . . a baby. I was six months into my pregnancy. It's safe to say, that wasn't exactly the "big" plans I had in mind. The discovery came with a lot of heartache, grief, and questioning why God would bring my dreams of a fresh start and new life tumbling down. I had no idea His plans would be so much better than I'd imagined.

I think the Lord puts us in situations where we cannot succeed without Him. He loves when the provision is so abundant and the deliverance so miraculous that no one can deny it's from Him. So when He's removing what makes you comfortable, you can trust that it's not preceding your defeat, but His victory.

I love what God said to Gideon about the army he would bring to war with the Midianites. The Lord allowed tens of thousands of soldiers in the Israelites' army to voluntarily retreat, then He ensured that all who were left were willing and prepared. I so appreciate this reminder that the Lord utilized and equipped those who were confident, even when the opposing army was larger and should have easily overcome them. God used those who were willing in faith to achieve a supernatural victory that would be impossible for them to take credit for.

Have you seen the Lord do this in your life? Throw a curveball you weren't expecting, and remove you from a place where you felt confident in your own ability to succeed? In these seasons the Enemy will tempt you to become self-conscious. He'll tempt you to isolate. He might tempt you to jump into boss mode and take control over whatever you can to ensure nothing is out of your hands. Where is the Enemy attacking you today?

Saying yes to God might feel like you're one of the final few soldiers facing the Midianites, but the victory is already guaranteed. Rather than praying your way out of your situation today, pray your way *into* it, and ask God what He wants to do in or through you. He'll show you.

Heavenly Father, thank You for reminding me that the battle has already been won. It feels like I'm facing an army on my own, and to be honest, I already feel defeated. Help me to walk in confidence of Your victory and to have the faith and trust that will say yes to Your call, even when I'm outnumbered. In Jesus' name, amen.

65
The Word Prepares Your Way

This Book of the Law shall not depart from your mouth, but you shall meditate on it day and night, so that you may be careful to do according to all that is written in it. For then you will make your way prosperous, and then you will have good success.

Joshua 1:8

I have a friend who is *so* incredibly talented. And yet her limiting beliefs hinder her. Did you know that limiting beliefs are just lies from the Enemy? He wants you to believe anything *but* the truth that God has good things for you, and He has perfectly equipped you to walk in them *today*. I've watched this friend, with more potential than many women I know, convince herself that she's not good enough—at the same time she's watching women far less qualified on paper walk in absolute joy, abundance, and favor simply because of their faith.

Now, you might be thinking, *Sarah, I do have faith in God, just not in myself.* Friend, don't you see that's the same thing?

How much more abundant would your life be if you were speaking out the truth of what God says about you, rather than repeating the lies the Enemy has planted that you've allowed to take root in your mind? Sister, we can't just speak out God's Word and hope the Enemy hears. We have to declare it so loudly that not only does the

Enemy hear it, but it drowns out his lies entirely. You have that power. You have access to this truth. Why not walk in this authority?

The Word of the Lord does not bend. We can build our lives on it and trust that it will remain firm. This is our only hope in carrying out the calling God has for our lives. It's through His Word that we learn His voice and His character. We see what He's done in the past, knowing we serve the same God who can do it again in the future. But we're not called to just digest it for ourselves; we're called to read it and not let it depart from our mouths, as we see in today's scripture.

Reading the Word equips you to hear, discern, and confirm God's voice. We know that His plans for us are better than we can imagine, right? So if you want to be prosperous, know the Word and live by it. Your abundance is a promise if you walk in the calling God has for you. But in order to follow His voice, you must know what it sounds like. Pursue the Lord and ask Him specifically what you need to walk into or away from.

Heavenly Father, thank You for the gift of Your Word. Help me to continuously go back to it as I look for direction and confirmation of Your plan. I want to hear Your voice and prosper in the plans You have for me. In Jesus' name, amen.

66

Discipline Is Like Watering Your Garden

For the moment all discipline seems painful rather than pleasant, but later it yields the peaceful fruit of righteousness to those who have been trained by it.

Hebrews 12:11

My flesh and my ego so badly desire to be seen. But over the last few years I've felt like I've been in an "unseen" season. What I've noticed the Lord teaching me through this is the discipline of staying faithful, even when others don't recognize my work or there is no reward.

Something God repeatedly brought to my attention was this piece of wisdom: "Seeds on a shelf don't become flowers." He revealed that the "seeds" were my God-given gifts, talents, and skills. And the flowers were the overflow of abundance, the fruit of my labor after staying faithful to plant, water, and weed the soil. In a humbling, convicting revelation, I realized that I had neglected planting the seeds for so long because that would require them to be *unseen*—even if just for a season. As I began asking God to work in me, I planted these seeds and watched Him grow them into a harvest that was so much more abundant than anything I could have produced on my own.

Doing anything other than what your flesh desires will likely feel difficult for a time. Just like when you start (or restart) working out, everything you do will feel foreign and painful. As you progress, the weights that once felt heavy will feel lighter, and you'll add to what you're lifting to increase your strength. But if you take some time off and then jump back in, the weights you were lifting before will feel heavy again. Strength requires consistency.

So many of us make excuses to put off being disciplined in working out, even though we feel so much better afterward, and we want the results it brings. Prayer is the same way. In order to see the growth the Lord wants to bring to fruition in your life, you must stay faithful in prayer and discipline. Prayer plants the seeds, discipline waters them, and refinement prunes the plant to remove what's hindering your growth.

Stay planted where the Lord has you until He moves you, and you will flourish. If you want a change, pray. But pray for His will, and be aware He may want to change you—even if it's in an unseen place for a time—before He changes your circumstance.

Heavenly Father, I want to grow in discipline so I can clearly differentiate between what You're leading me to and what just satisfies my flesh. I don't want to stay comfortable in any ways that limit my growth. Thank You for the assurance that my consistency will bear fruit. In Jesus' name, amen.

STAY FAITHFUL IN PRAYER

67

Pray So You Can Be Prepared

"If it pleases the king, let letters be given me to the governors of the province Beyond the River, that they may let me pass through until I come to Judah, and a letter to Asaph, the keeper of the king's forest, that he may give me timber to make beams for the gates of the fortress of the temple, and for the wall of the city, and for the house that I shall occupy." And the king granted me what I asked, for the good hand of my God was upon me.

Nehemiah 2:7–8

When Harv was just an itty-bitty baby, I found myself on my face before the altar at church, with him strapped to my chest. This was a regular occurrence in this season, as I was desperate for a move of God and so tired of waiting on manna to survive. On this particular evening, I felt a hand on my back, and a woman began to pray over me with words I'll never forget. She prayed that God would increase my faith and that I would have boldness to request things that would only be possible in the supernatural. That I would live expectant of miracles. I later found out that woman was singer-songwriter Brooke Ligertwood. Her prayer changed the trajectory of my life, leading me to faithfully anticipate the *abundantly more* plans God had for me.

I think sometimes we don't pray and ask God for what we need because we know once we receive it, we'll be out of excuses and we'll have to *go*. But isn't the whole reason we're telling ourselves we're afraid to move forward because we don't know or have what we need? Prayer changes everything. Don't let fear of the unknown fuel you more than your faith in the future God has for you.

Nehemiah first asked God what he would need to walk in God's plans for him to rebuild the walls of Jerusalem. Then he asked for the *fullness* of what he would need, sparing no details or expense when given the opportunity. Do you ask for what you need with this much boldness?

Nehemiah didn't worry about being "too much," scaring the king with his requests, or stressing about how it was all going to come to pass. He asked for exactly what he needed.

God loves to show up where we expect Him to—and where we don't.

Heavenly Father, I want to seek You as boldly and intentionally as Nehemiah did. I want to have no fear when asking for what I need to carry out Your plan. Help me be a vessel that points other people to You, through my own faith and obedience. I ask for an abundance, so I can give in abundance. In Jesus' name, amen.

68

His Word Will Light
Your Next Step

Your word is a lamp to my feet and a light to my path.

Psalm 119:105

When I was a kid, my parents loved to take my siblings and me camping. We lived in steamy Florida, so we'd fall asleep sweaty, wake up dripping in condensation, and if we were lucky, we'd make it past day two without raccoons breaking into our coolers and stealing our food.

The worst part, though, was having to get up in the middle of the night when nature called, walking through the pitch black, using only a lantern to light the path just ahead. We could see the glow of the bathhouse in the distance and trusted that our lanterns would reveal anything in our path we needed to stay away from.

It's a well-known analogy that the Word of God is like those lanterns: illuminating only the next step or two. Not too far ahead, just enough to know we're not going to stumble on anything in our path. Isn't that so true? I think it's easy to believe the lie that unless we have a floodlight and can see every single inch of what's ahead, we shouldn't move forward. But be honest, if you saw the fullness of God's plan for you, do you think you'd move forward, knowing what you were getting yourself into? I probably wouldn't!

If I'd had the option to avoid divorce and single motherhood, I would have opted out, 100 percent. But now that I'm on the other side, and I have seen how God strengthened me and provided for me through it all, I'd do it again in a heartbeat. God, in His goodness, protects us from seeing something that we would avoid if we thought we didn't have the strength to navigate it. In reality, the whole time God was planning on supernaturally delivering us through it. I'd rather let the unknown fuel my faith than let what's out of my control fuel my fear.

If your time in the Word is what's lighting your path, how bright is it? God wants our lamp lit bright enough to discern if there's anything in our path that might cause us to stumble! But you'll only have this clarity if you're in the Word consistently so you can identify what is, and isn't, from Him. Spend intentional time with Jesus and memorize His Word so your path stays lit.

Heavenly Father, thank You for Your Word and the insight it gives me to Your heart. Help me to go to You every single day in preparation for my day, not in response to it. I want to be equipped with exactly what I need to face the journey You have for me. I surrender my plan for Yours. In Jesus' name, amen.

69

Intimacy Before Impact

And he said to him, "You shall love the Lord your God with all your heart and with all your soul and with all your mind. This is the great and first commandment."

Matthew 22:37-38

My husband and I are similar in many ways, but in others our wiring couldn't be more opposite. What comes naturally to me is not at all what he needs, and vice versa. Even though it takes a lot of intentionality to connect with him, it brings me joy. I look forward to hearing what's on his mind; I trust him with my deepest, darkest secrets; I check in with him often and run my plans and ideas by him to show him that I honor and value his perspective. *Because I love him.*

Loving the Lord is the greatest commandment Jesus gave, but do you treat Him like someone you love? Singer-songwriter Steffany Gretzinger has said that many of us claim to love God, but we treat Him like a stranger passing by. We keep the conversation surface level, and we don't hold space or seem interested in more than just an acknowledgement of His presence. Convicting, isn't it?

When you love someone, you check in often, right? It's not just a one-time thing or a one-way conversation. You want to hear their deepest thoughts and desires. You keep their words in the forefront of your mind, wanting to honor them and show how much you care. You connect with them regularly, coordinate plans with them, and ask them for guidance when you don't know what to do next. Does your relationship with the Lord look like this?

God gave you the desire to live a life of purpose, influence, and abundance for a reason. I know it's easy sometimes to feel as if those dreams are like a carrot being dangled in front of a horse. Like no matter how many steps forward you take, the prize is still that much farther away. Maybe you're afraid to bring your dreams before the Lord because you're afraid He'll tell you *no*. The Enemy wants us to believe that walking in the Lord's plan is preventing our own, but that couldn't be further from the truth. God first desires intimacy with you before He will use you for impact.

When you pursue God before anything else, He'll take care of everything else. Prioritize your time with the Lord and sit with Him in your quiet place. What He does through you will never be more important than what He does in you.

Heavenly Father, thank You for the blessing of being in relationship with You. Help me to draw near to You, even when I feel like running away or shutting down. I love You and want to trust You with my most vulnerable dreams, desires, and disappointments. I receive the fullness You have for me. In Jesus' name, amen.

70

Your Setback Might Be Your Success

It has become known throughout the whole imperial guard and to all the rest that my imprisonment is for Christ. And most of the brothers, having become confident in the Lord by my imprisonment, are much more bold to speak the word without fear.

Philippians 1:13–14

My friend Hope Reagan Harris's life is a constant, convicting reminder to me of how purpose can be found even through what feels like imprisonment. Hope was offered her dream job, only for the offer to be rescinded when she was on maternity leave. Here she was, a new mom, experiencing postpartum depression, and then the loss of a potential job—and she found herself asking God why He'd take away what she had worked so hard for. Then God began revealing that what He had for her was so much bigger.

The same day Hope resolved to be at peace in the midst of her confusion, she received an email for a job with a platform that had shaped her life spiritually in a massive way. Suddenly, it all made sense. Her purpose was revealed in a way she couldn't have imagined. So often our purpose is revealed only through our ability to part with our plans.

Walking in the fullness God has for you is not dependent on your success but on how you glorify Him in your struggle. The Enemy wants you so focused on the fact that life isn't going the way you planned, you don't even realize it's going exactly the way the Lord has planned.

Can you imagine being Paul? He left his old life behind to follow Christ and preach the good news, only to get thrown in jail. If it were me, I'd probably feel pretty defeated, even embarrassed. Thoughts would race through my mind like, *What does this say about the God I've been preaching, that He'd repay me by letting me be thrown in prison? Why would anyone else decide to follow this God?*

Is that how you're feeling today? Maybe you, like Paul, have served and sacrificed for years, only to end up in what feels like your own prison. I invite you to consider that maybe the circumstances you think are holding you back are actually exactly what God will use to propel you forward.

The Lord is using you in the areas you feel imprisoned to refine you, and He will use you in powerful ways you never would have experienced if life had gone according to your plan. Your purpose here on earth is to make disciples, and the abundance you receive through your obedience is the joy of knowing you're walking in that purpose.

Dear heavenly Father, thank You for reminding me that there's purpose in every season, even the ones that feel like a prison. Give me peace surrounding what I have not accomplished and can't control, and boldness to share Your goodness even when I feel far from it. In Jesus' name, amen.

71

Preparation for the Harvest

Do not be deceived: God is not mocked, for whatever one sows, that will he also reap.

Galatians 6:7

There was a season in my life when God was promising to do "abundantly more" than I could ask or imagine, yet I was barely scraping by. I was encouraging others that He would do something incredible in their lives, yet I was struggling to believe it for myself. I felt like such a fraud.

I started questioning whether I'd really heard God right. "Why is nothing working out the way I had planned, God? Did I misunderstand?" Then He whispered something that changed my life: *The preparation isn't going according to your plans because I'm going to do something bigger than you could imagine.* I was in a season of preparation. At the time, it looked like a season of trial and disappointment. But over time, I began to see it was a season of refinement, and the Lord needed me to go through that before lifting me up into opportunities I couldn't have worked hard enough to earn.

Our "progress" means nothing to God. He doesn't measure progress like the world does. He observes our preparation.

The preparation the Lord leads you through might not make sense to you. Maybe you fear that you're not far enough along to accomplish your dreams. Or you doubt your own ability. Or you haven't seen the progress you think you need to get where you're going. I want to stop you right there. Rebuke the lie from the Enemy that you're not "further along" because you're not enough, and rest in the promise that the Lord sees your heart, your obedience, and your dreams.

If you're in a season of preparation, like I was, don't be discouraged; the harvest season will come eventually, and the purpose of this season will soon be revealed. For now, see this time as preparation while you wait for the harvest. Wake up every morning ready to walk in obedience to what He's calling you into, and if you can't clearly see what that looks like just yet, *sow seeds*.

Sister, your purpose is right in front of you. You don't have to be afraid of being left behind or not progressing because you're not pushing forward. God gave you the dreams and desires you hold, and He will bring them to fruition for His glory in due time.

Heavenly Father, help me to rest in Your promises today. If I'm honest, I'm getting tired of sowing seeds without reaping the harvest I want so badly. Help me to find joy in this season You have me in, and show me how I can steward this season well. In Jesus' name, amen.

YOUR PURPOSE IS RIGHT IN FRONT OF YOU

72

The Wilderness Is Not a Punishment

[Satan] said to him, "If you are the Son of God, throw yourself down, for it is written, 'He will command his angels concerning you,' and 'On their hands they will bear you up, lest you strike your foot against a stone.'" Jesus said to him, "Again it is written, 'You shall not put the Lord your God to the test.'"

Matthew 4:6–7

My sister Jamey is my hero. She is a year and a half younger than me, and she was a single foster mom to teenage girls *and* their babies for two years. Every day was a battle as she had to navigate the emotional, spiritual, and even physical challenges that came with teenagers who had experienced trauma. So many times she felt like throwing in the towel, but she continuously called upon the Lord for strength. Over and over, He poured out His grace and gave her the peace and discernment she needed to face another day. But man, it was not easy.

This was her wilderness. A season where many questioned her for stepping into it, but she knew God had called her. She even broke up with a guy who advised against it (I never liked him to start with!).

Jamey recently completed her last day as a foster mom, and the Lord has already flung new doors and opportunities wide open.

Did you know that Jesus went to the wilderness out of obedience? Matthew 4 records His encounter where Satan kept tempting Him. It wasn't a punishment. Jesus was sinless and had nothing to be punished for. Jesus was fully aware that He would be physically vulnerable and tempted by the Enemy in the wilderness. God was asking Him to be obedient as He faced the Enemy.

How would your spiritual life look different if you woke up every morning, put on your armor, and prepared to face the Enemy? What if doing so made you quicker to recognize his antics to distract you or get you off course? Knowing you might face the Enemy in a wilderness doesn't necessarily make your encounter with him easier, but having that knowledge will help you to be on high alert and be quicker to rebuke the lies he will whisper.

God will guide you if you seek Him and familiarize yourself with His voice. The Enemy's lies may sound close to the truth, but they will only satisfy your flesh rather than your spirit. Ask the Lord to reveal where you can deny your flesh to more clearly hear His voice.

Heavenly Father, help me to be so familiar with Your voice that I recognize when it's not Yours, even when it sounds like what I want to hear. Forgive me for all the times I also expected You to prove Yourself, as if You're not the same God yesterday, today, and forever. In Jesus' name, amen.

73

Gratitude and Anxiety Can't Coexist

Do not be anxious about anything, but in everything
by prayer and supplication with thanksgiving
let your requests be made known to God.

Philippians 4:6

After David and I remarried, I felt elated that God would be so kind to answer so many prayers abundantly. Except for one thing: I didn't have a job. I kept trusting that God would provide, but David's job change had proven not to be what we expected, and I needed something *fast*. I spent hours looking for jobs online, racing against the clock and our automatic payments. I was filled with anxiety and felt guilty that no matter how hard I tried, I couldn't get a call back. Panic started to set in.

I prayed, *God, I don't care what You have for me. I will do it. I'll do anything. But please, make a way for us, Lord.* After a few days of hearing nothing but crickets in response, the Holy Spirit dropped it on my heart to check in with a friend and offer to help with her social media so I could be using my gifts to serve someone while I waited. Within three weeks, my one act of service turned into fourteen clients, simply from word of mouth. God had opened the floodgates!

The Bible says don't be anxious about *anything*. Did you catch that? I know you probably feel like your situation is dire enough to be anxious about. You might think, *If you only knew what I'm walking through, you'd understand.* Girl, I *do* understand! I also know there is absolutely nothing worth your peace. God loves to show up. But if you're so busy focusing on the problem, you'll miss the provision.

With *everything*, pray. There's nothing too big and nothing too small for the Lord. He loves to bring the desires of our heart to fruition, and He loves to shape those desires to reflect *His*. That's why He tells us to pray about everything.

The Enemy doesn't want you to know that *your brain cannot hold thanksgiving and anxiety at the same time.* You have to choose one. You can be paralyzed by fear, or you can walk forward in faith. Worship displaces doubt. Praise Him for who He is, what He's done, and what you believe He will do. Leave room for nothing other than gratitude to infiltrate your prayers and requests to God.

Heavenly Father, thank You for encouraging me to bring my requests to You. Help me to surrender the areas where I'm feeling anxious to You today. I don't want anything to distract me from what You're leading me into. In Jesus' name, amen.

74

Your Life Is Your Worship

I appeal to you therefore, brothers, by the mercies of God, to present your bodies as a living sacrifice, holy and acceptable to God, which is your spiritual worship.

Romans 12:1

I remember sitting in church one Sunday after a particularly rough week. I was wrestling with imposter syndrome and had spent days in isolation, feeling unworthy and avoiding some opportunities that were totally out of my comfort zone. There at church, I was singing that God was worthy of all the glory when I heard Him say, *If I'm worthy of it, why are you acting like it's dependent on you?* I almost choked! I couldn't believe He called me out like that. The more I thought about it, the more convicted I became. How could I say He was worthy while doubting what He could do in and through me?

Your spiritual worship is not just how you treat others, but how you treat yourself. If you're anything like me, you frequently put others' needs first and push your needs to the back burner. This is something a lot of my friends and sisters in the Abundantly More Community talk about. We put ourselves down, or claim we're not good enough—practicing "false humility," which isn't actually humility but a denial of our worth. Often, I hear women justify this by quoting Jesus: "Love your neighbor as yourself" (Mark 12:31). But can I point something out? The scripture says to love your neighbor *as* yourself, not *better than* yourself.

God wants what you have to offer. It's your way of worshiping Him. Ask God to reveal where you need to better steward what He's entrusted to you, so that every step you take is another seed sown that will reap a bountiful harvest. Your calling is not walked out just in how you navigate the big things, but also in how you move through the things that seem small enough to avoid without anyone noticing. It's usually those things that make the biggest impact in your life, and in the lives of others.

To receive the fullness of God's plan, we need to exercise the fullness of the faith required to walk in it. We may want an increase of abundance, opportunity, finances, or health, but we neglect the opportunity He's given us to steward what we currently have well. How you use your gifts on a small scale is exactly how you'll use them on a large scale. And the Lord will allow you to refine these skills before elevating you to a level that would just bring overwhelm if you weren't ready. Don't mistake this as a "waiting" season. It's a preparation season.

Heavenly Father, thank You for creating me with a purpose and for desiring a relationship with Me. Help me to steward the calling You're given me well, and to view obedience to what You're calling me into as my worship. In Jesus' name, amen.

75

Your Fruit Will Outlast Your Fame

"You did not choose me, but I chose you and appointed you that you should go and bear fruit and that your fruit should abide, so that whatever you ask the Father in my name, he may give it to you."

John 15:16

I usually see the Lord call me where I feel least equipped.

What about you?

Walking in the fullness that God has for you is not a matter of whether you're qualified or equipped, but whether you'll say yes to the call. Maybe saying yes is a struggle because whatever God is asking of you feels so far out of your comfort zone, you're having a hard time even believing it's from Him. Or maybe you can't imagine He would want you to use your time, energy, and resources on something you don't have a perfectly executed plan for, right?

"You did not choose me, but I chose you" (John 15:16). Jesus' words shift my perspective from feeling like I get to pick and choose when I obey, to remembering that God chose me and put me on this earth for a reason. So if He's calling me into something, there's a purpose bigger than I can see—and it has nothing to do with whether I feel ready.

When we walk in our own strength, we might make an impact, find success, and have our name remembered. But when we're filled with the Holy Spirit, our fruit far outlasts the impact and legacy of our own success. When we ask the Holy Spirit to equip us, the fruit of the Spirit isn't just for us; it's for us to share. And God is much more interested in our fruit than our fame.

I'll never forget the day I was venting to my dad about how overwhelmed I was juggling everything on my plate: motherhood, writing a book, building a business, being a new wife, navigating a move, taxes (ugh), and so on. He heard the discouragement in my voice and responded, "You weren't put on this earth to be overwhelmed. You know that, right?" My pride wanted to defend myself. And for a split second I almost lost it on him! But the Lord quickly humbled me, and I realized he was right.

Your calling was never meant to be a burden. If it feels like one, you're probably trying to carry it in your own strength. Surrender the lie that you're behind or you've failed, and ask the Lord what He wants to do in you or through you here. He chose you. He'll walk with you.

Heavenly Father, thank You for not expecting me to carry the weight of my calling alone. Help me to surrender the overwhelm I feel in this season to You and to walk in the plans You have for me with boldness. Please give me eyes to see how You want to work in and through me. In Jesus' name, amen.

76

Give, and Watch What You Receive

"If I then, your Lord and Teacher, have washed your feet, you also ought to wash one another's feet. For I have given you an example, that you also should do just as I have done to you."

John 13:14–15

An author and speaker I respect very much named John Maxwell once said, "If you're too big to serve, you're too small to lead." As someone who loves to lead, that has stuck with me and, not surprisingly, proven to be true. I've always wanted to establish trust based on my ability to "get the job done." I want to get it done efficiently, without mistakes, and with as little hassle as possible on the other person's end.

What I've noticed recently, though, as motherhood has humbled me and I've been forced to pull the "I have no idea what I'm doing" card more than once, is that people actually care less about you having it all together and more about your willingness to simply serve.

When I stopped being a greeter at church (a very important job full of outward rewards, like meeting new people and exchanging smiles with fellow worshipers) and started picking up trash and keeping the nursery stocked with diapers and wipes, I was amazed at how many people appreciated my willingness to serve in a less-than-glamorous role. I realized quickly that being the best isn't as important as being willing.

Time and time again, I've watched the Lord confirm how He rewards those who simply obey Him, regardless of what's required. I want to be known as someone who says yes to His instruction—especially when it entails serving someone and being a reflection of Jesus. Don't you?

God will fill us to the capacity that we pour out. Jesus gave us the example of washing each other's feet (John 13). He wants us to serve each other freely, more concerned about meeting a need than preserving our energy for our own provision. When we serve, we receive blessing in return. Live as though everything you give, you'll also receive. Do it for the purpose of being an extension of Christ.

"Do just as I have done to you."

Heavenly Father, thank You for setting the example by first serving us. Help me to walk in generosity and humility so that I can fulfill the purpose You created me for. Give me eyes to see where I can love others and help them feel Your love through me. In Jesus' name, amen.

GOD IS PRESENT EVEN IN THE STORM

77

The Calm in the Storm

A great windstorm arose, and the waves were breaking into the boat, so that the boat was already filling. But he was in the stern, asleep on the cushion. And they woke him and said to him, "Teacher, do you not care that we are perishing?" And he awoke and rebuked the wind and said to the sea, "Peace! Be still!" And the wind ceased, and there was a great calm. He said to them, "Why are you so afraid? Have you still no faith?"

Mark 4:37–40

As I mentioned earlier, when I was five months postpartum and single, I found a journal that I had kept when David and I were first married. I sobbed as I flipped through the pages and remembered so much heartache and pain. I read through years of entries where I was begging God to change my husband, asking Him to drastically change our marriage. As I read what I had written in the journal and relived that incredibly hopeless, scary season, I was brought to my knees asking God in that moment, "Why did I have to go through this, Lord? Especially just for it to end?"

Suddenly, I turned to a page with a revelation I had forgotten in the chaos of divorce, an unplanned pregnancy, and single motherhood. It read, "Lord, forgive me. I've been praying and begging You to change my husband and change my circumstances, but what

I think You really wanted to change this whole time was me." In both seasons God was far less interested in removing me from the storm than He was in using it to refine me. That reminder gave me a renewed perspective that the storms we encounter in life are God's way of preparing us, not punishing us.

Oftentimes God uses a storm to take us places in our faith we've never been before. There's no denying your storm is real and the threat is intimidating. It may have you paralyzed in fear or anxious about when you'll feel safe and secure again. Your mind was designed to protect you. So no matter how big or small this storm is, if it's something you've never walked through before or is outside of your comfort zone that it will register as huge, maybe even the equivalent to death, in your mind.

Maybe you feel like God has called you out just to leave you stranded. You're crying out to Him in the middle of your storm, assuming He doesn't care. You don't see Him, and you definitely can't hear Him, so you're convinced He's abandoned you. It's understandable why you might be panicking in the unknown right now. But the storm raging around you does not mean God isn't with you.

Just like Jesus was with the disciples in the midst of their storm (Mark 4), God is with you in the midst of yours. Trust Him.

Heavenly Father, thank You for inviting me to come to You when I am afraid. I know You have a bigger plan than what I'm walking through right now. Please help me trust You in the middle of my storms. In Jesus' name, amen.

78

Nothing to Fear

And the satraps, the prefects, the governors, and the
king's counselors gathered together and saw that the
fire had not had any power over the bodies of those men.
The hair of their heads was not singed, their cloaks were
not harmed, and no smell of fire had come upon them.

Daniel 3:27

When I felt God tell me to turn down the job offer that would guarantee the financial security I needed, I was scared. I was so tired of struggling to make ends meet, and more than that, I was afraid of what people would think of me for turning down a job with nothing else lined up. But because radical faith had been required to sell everything to get to where I was, I knew it would all be for nothing if I turned back at that point. So I declined the job and prayed—harder than I ever had before!—that God would make a way.

Sure enough, not even a week later I was offered the perfect little home for Harv and me. That meant that instead of being kept busy with the job I turned down, I entered a season of stillness and supernatural provision.

If you're looking at your current circumstances or the season ahead, dreading the effects it will have on you or your future or what others will say about you, let me encourage you with the story of Shadrach, Meshach, and Abednego (Daniel 3).

These three men refused to bow down and worship anyone but their God. As a result, they were thrown into a furnace so hot that the guards who shut the door fell dead. But, God. He came through. He met them when they were helpless. He changed their story. And everyone who was there witnessed not just their resistance to the fire, but how they were joined by an angel. As they were released from the flame, onlookers stared in awe as Shadrach, Meshach, and Abednego were completely unharmed. Not even the smell of smoke followed them.

In the same way, God's deliverance is not just for you. It's for the witnesses to your life and your story too. You have no clue how many people will hear your story and be impacted by the faithfulness of God. Also, like these heroes of the faith, your faith won't return void. No matter how unfair your situation, there's a greater purpose. And if you have God's fire *in* you, you won't be afraid of the fire around you.

You have nothing to fear. Wake up and ask God, "What do You have for me today?"

Heavenly Father, help me to trust You as I'm walking through the fire, believing that I'll emerge completely unharmed. I struggle with feeling discouraged when my circumstances feel so defeating and unfair. Please give me strength and supernatural faith in Your deliverance. In Jesus' name, amen.

79

Faith Larger Than Your Circumstances

"Take your son, your only son Isaac, whom you love, and go to the land of Moriah, and offer him there as a burnt offering . . . . So Abraham rose early in the morning, saddled his donkey, and took two of his young men with him, and his son Isaac. And he cut the wood for the burnt offering and arose and went to the place of which God had told him.

Genesis 22:2-3

Has God ever told you to do something, and it was the last thing you wanted to do? This is often the way it goes between God and me. He has repeatedly called me to the very thing I don't want to do with every fiber of my being. It usually looks like practicing patience, giving my precious time to serve, stepping out of my comfort zone totally in faith, or extending forgiveness and love to someone difficult.

What about you? How creative have you gotten trying to buy yourself more time, because you know better than to say no, but you're terrified to say yes? Maybe God has called you to start a business or ministry, lay something down, forgive someone, or start tithing . . . and you've been dragging your feet.

When I was in this spot, the Lord spoke to me through the story of Abraham and Isaac (Genesis 22). God told Abraham to sacrifice his son Isaac, and Abraham didn't just obey halfheartedly. When he traveled to the land of Moriah to perform the sacrifice, Abraham brought servants, donkeys, plenty of wood, and other materials he would need. He didn't go kicking and screaming; he walked in bold faith that this call to obedience was for something much greater than what made sense in that moment. And after Abraham made his way up the mountain, prepared the altar, and lifted the knife to take his own son's life, the Lord delivered a ram to take Isaac's place.

When I read that, I'm reminded that God's plans are bigger than we can know, and He asks for our obedience in the unknown. He asks that we show up, that we seek Him, that we obey Him. If Abraham had not carried out the Lord's order fully, he may have never received the deliverance the Lord had in store all along.

I want to challenge you today to take inventory of the things the Lord has placed on your heart that you've put off. Whether you've done so because you're afraid, or you just didn't think you were ready, I want to encourage you to write them down and ask Him what He wants you to take action on. God will provide for you as you move forward in faith. Ask Him where you need to be obedient, and then walk as though the provision is already in place.

Heavenly Father, thank You for going before me and preparing me with all that I need to be victorious. Forgive me for playing small, or only meeting You halfway because I'm afraid of stepping out completely in faith. Help me to obey, confident of Your ability rather than my own. In Jesus' name, amen.

80

The Lord Elevates You, Not Your Experience

Then Samuel said to Jesse, "Are all your sons here?" And he said, "There remains yet the youngest, but behold, he is keeping the sheep." And Samuel said to Jesse, "Send and get him, for we will not sit down till he comes here."

1 Samuel 16:11

When Harv and I got our first place *alone*, it was in the middle of nowhere, with my closest friends being forty-five minutes away. As a social butterfly, this was my nightmare. Over time, I began to recognize it wasn't a punishment. It had a purpose. I was entering my "hidden" season. During that time, I felt called to steward what was right in front of me: my neighbors, my child, my online community, and more. As my heart shifted toward stewardship rather than a busy social life or massive job success, my endurance grew. My patience grew. My faith even grew. I started trusting that God had a plan bigger than the season I was in—and I believed He was good even if the journey didn't make sense or the outcome wasn't what I wanted.

Sure enough, exactly a year after we'd moved in, God snatched me right out of my little mobile home in Bon Aqua, Tennessee, and began the process of reconciliation between David and me. This was the last thing I thought I was being prepared for, but it turned out even better than what I could have imagined.

Do you feel like you're in a hidden season? I know it's so tough when the world tells you that if you don't have a detailed five-year plan, you shouldn't expect much from life. If you're feeling discouraged about your future because of where you are right now, listen, sister: *obedience is what prepares you for the Lord's plan for your life*, not your experience or strategy.

Consider Jesse's son David. When Samuel asked to see Jesse's sons, David's dad brought out every single one of his brothers who were tall, strong, handsome, and seemingly equipped to be king. But God told Samuel none of them would become king. When Samuel asked if there were any others, Jesse hedged, "Yeah, one, but he's just out tending to the sheep." Lo and behold, when Samuel saw David, he knew this ruddy boy was the one appointed to be king.

David was being prepared to be king as a shepherd. He had his own version of a hidden season. Obedience in an unseen season may be preparing you for a position higher than you think, or an outcome you can't imagine, and God will send people on His behalf to offer you the opportunities, provision, or resources you need. Focus on being faithful and trust God with the rest.

Heavenly Father, help me to trust in Your provision today. Sometimes I feel like I'm in a season of being unnoticed, or I feel like the work I'm doing isn't important. I know that in Your perfect timing, You'll open the doors for what's next. I don't want to waste a single second of the preparation season You have me in. In Jesus' name, amen.

81

The Lord Will Renew Your Strength

They who wait for the LORD shall renew their strength;
they shall mount up with wings like eagles; they shall
run and not be weary; they shall walk and not faint.

Isaiah 40:31

I'll never forget sitting on my couch, in the living room of the mobile home where I lived with Harv, begging God through tears for something to shift. I was at my wits' end in every way possible. As I shared earlier, I had just gotten a depression diagnosis, my bank account was negative, Harv wasn't sleeping through the night, and I needed a move of God that would radically change my circumstances if I had any hope of survival.

I kept hearing the scripture, "In due time, I the Lord will make it happen" (Isaiah 60:22, my paraphrase). What an encouraging thought, right? No. This was actually even more discouraging! Couldn't God see that the time was *now*? I journaled all of my frustration about God's timing, knowing I would be able to look back at His faithfulness to deliver me. But in that moment I was so weary.

I went to bed and woke the next morning to a text that had some life-changing news. I found out I'd received an opportunity to do something professionally that was beyond my wildest dreams. It was unexpected and unplanned—and not something I could have ever made happen. It was . . . well, it was "in due time." With God, circumstances can change in an instant.

In my frustration, in my weariness in the waiting, I could only wait for God to move. In due time. In *His* time. If you're feeling worn out or burnt out, wait on the Lord. He will give you strength to walk in what He has for you. And even if you don't know how it will play out, you can take comfort that He will be with you. That He has a plan, and you're not alone, left to wander.

Too often we claim we're looking for God's will without being honest with ourselves that it's really *our* will that we're seeking. In those cases we're waiting on confirmation that will never come, because God has something else in store for us.

What is God calling you to in this season, and what are you waiting on before you start walking in that calling? Are you limiting yourself based on who you think *you* are, or who you think *God* is? Where does your confidence come from?

If you don't know what is next, if you're in a season of waiting, talk to Him. Ask Him what to do next. While you wait for your calling or even your next small step, you can rest in His strength.

Heavenly Father, thank You for the gift of getting to cast my burdens onto You. Thank You for not creating me to carry this calling alone but to lean on You when I need a renewal of strength. That's where I am today, Lord. Give me grace for myself and others. In Jesus' name, amen.

HE WILL GIVE YOU STRENGTH

82

The Fruit of Your Faithfulness

"Abide in me, and I in you. As the branch cannot
bear fruit by itself, unless it abides in the vine,
neither can you, unless you abide in me."

John 15:4

I'm the worst plant mom ever. I'll make mental notes to water a plant, then forget and slowly watch it wither. Sometimes I'll remember to care for it and watch it perk up a little, only to see it wither again from a lack of adequate water and sunlight.

As believers, we're like delicate plants that sometimes flourish and sometimes wither. If you're anything like me, you live your life running as fast as you can and as far as you can without stopping for fuel. You're quick to tend to the needs of others, throwing yourself into ministries and saying yes to every opportunity, trying to be everything to everyone—a mom, friend, sister, spiritual mentor, cook, cleaner, or whatever anyone else needs. Then when you realize you're running on E, you prioritize spending time in the Word for long enough to perk up a little, only to find yourself running on fumes again. You too? Or is it just me?

The Lord doesn't require us to hustle for the fullness He has for us. He doesn't want us to run on fumes or wait to be replenished till we've completely run dry. Branches bear fruit when they simply stay connected to the vine. The same is true for you with Christ. When you're regularly spending time with God, seeking Him in all aspects of your life and throughout your day, your fruitfulness will naturally overflow out of your faithfulness.

You might be tempted to pursue the *fruit* rather than the *connection*. It's our human nature to want success more than we want what God really desires—for us to be patient, vulnerable, and dependent on Him. I often look for the fastest way to accomplish something to reach my goals more efficiently, rather than pausing to make sure I'm connected to God and His will. If your desire for the results trumps your desire for relationship, you'll find yourself taking shortcuts that will not only result in counterfeit fruit, but a disconnect from God.

Only the fruit that comes from God will lead you to the life He has for you. But you can't have the fruit without being connected to the vine. This season may be a chance for you to get in the consistent habit of asking the Holy Spirit to equip you with what you need to move forward. It may be a season of staying faithful and watching for the fruit that is coming. If you stay connected to the source, the fruit will come.

Heavenly Father, thank You for being a constant source that I can rely on for the strength to more forward. Help me to seek You and walk in the fruit of the Spirit rather than pursuing my own goals or choosing my own response. I want others to see You when they see me, and I want my life to be fully surrendered to Your plan. In Jesus' name, amen.

Trust God in the Unknown

Therefore, my beloved brothers, be steadfast, immovable, always abounding in the work of the Lord, knowing that in the Lord your labor is not in vain.

1 Corinthians 15:58

When Enaka, the woman who would become my best friend, took a leap of faith to move with me to Nashville, we'd never even met face-to-face! We had only recently connected on social media.

Even though the arrangement was technically her idea, I don't think she expected me to jump on board and get the ball rolling so fast! What she did know was that God had put it on her heart to move. Despite all the unknowns, she packed up her car, signed a lease with me, and drove ten hours from her hometown in the DC area. It didn't make sense, but Enaka trusted God to provide, and she released her need to understand it all.

Shortly after moving to Nashville, she found herself immersed in an incredible church community and support system, boldly walking in her God-given gifts, and seeing her faith bear fruit through the Lord's provision. She trusted God's leading and sought Him in the unknown. And God had so much more in store for her!

When God calls us, it's so easy to prepare for the worst and limit our faith to survival mode, worrying about our security or the specific plans we have for ourselves. But God has so much more for us.

The future that the Lord has for you is so abundant, it's bigger than you could ever ask, think, or imagine. Because of this, the preparation may be beyond what you could comprehend. So if you're walking through a season that doesn't make sense, you can release the expectation to understand and walk by faith, trusting it's a part of His plan.

What He calls you to in this season won't necessarily look like "progress." Others may look on and question if what you're doing is "smart," "responsible," or even a good use of your time. There may be no road map or obvious return on investment. But stand firm in your faith and be bold in your obedience. This work is not for you; it's for the Lord.

Your brain is designed to keep you safe, so anything you've never done before will send an SOS signal, warning you to beware. If there is no guarantee of success, your brain might raise a caution flag. That's OK. If there's a voice in the back of your mind telling you to move forward even though it's completely out of your comfort zone, and if it keeps popping back up and tugging on your heart no matter how many times you push it down—it's probably the Lord!

Heavenly Father, thank You for reminding me that my labor is not in vain. I can get discouraged when time goes by and I don't see the results I want yet, so help me remember that my purpose isn't found in the outcome. It's developed on the journey. Equip me with the boldness to abound in Your work. In Jesus' name, amen.

84
God Can Use the Hurt

And he said, "I am your brother, Joseph, whom you
sold into Egypt. And now do not be distressed or
angry with yourselves because you sold me here,
for God sent me before you to preserve life. . . .
So it was not you who sent me here, but God."

Genesis 45:4–5, 8

After my divorce, I was bitter for a very long time. I believed I was a victim, and that belief held me captive. It wasn't until God opened my eyes to the chains that were keeping me in bondage that I realized I'd been missing the opportunity to walk in His plans. I was stuck because I was holding on to resentment toward my ex, the person I thought had robbed me of those plans. As I began to extend forgiveness toward David, the Lord not only softened my heart toward him, but even began stirring David's heart to pursue reconciliation. It's crazy to think that I would have never experienced what's been such a humbling, beautiful chapter had I not allowed God to use someone who hurt me to also heal me.

You may be believing the lie that something or someone else is responsible for where you are in life. You may think that if that person hadn't hurt you, if you hadn't been passed up for the job or opportunity, if you had a little more time and a lot more money, you'd be reaching your potential. Can I be real with you? Absolutely *nothing* and *no one* is powerful enough to keep you from what God has for you.

In the Old Testament, Joseph was tossed into a ditch and then sold into slavery by his own brothers. He worked hard to earn an elevated position, only to be falsely accused and then thrown in prison. Years later, he was released and appointed as a leader over Egypt. And when Egypt faced a food shortage, Joseph's brothers traveled to come before him and ask for food, not realizing they were asking their own brother, the very one they had sold into slavery years prior.

Can you even imagine? Joseph's response blows me away. He said, "Don't be angry with yourselves. It wasn't you who sent me here, but God." Convicting, huh? Joseph saw that God used their wrongdoing to not just *prepare* him for a position of power, but *lead* him to it. What his brothers had intended for his downfall ended up being what God used to elevate him beyond his wildest dreams.

Heavenly Father, thank You for holding my future in Your hands. Help me to release the bitterness I feel toward what has hindered me. I know that no one is powerful enough to take away what You have for me. Heal my heart, Lord, and open my eyes to see what You have for me in this season. In Jesus' name, amen.

85
The Blessing of Rock Bottom

"But whoever drinks of the water that I will give him will never be thirsty again. The water that I will give him will become in him a spring of water welling up to eternal life."

John 4:14

I've hit rock bottom more times than I can count. Probably because the Lord has a lot to teach me about surrendering control and being willing to receive what He has for me—instead of pushing myself to the point of burnout trying to earn it for myself. I'm learning that hitting rock bottom doesn't mean you've failed. It means the Lord has allowed you to reach the end of *your* resources so He can fill you with *His*.

The Enemy will try to make me feel both unworthy of what God is calling me into and overwhelmed by it. Time and time again, I watch myself crumble under the pressure, only to realize I've set a completely unrealistic expectation for myself, and that I've tried to carry the weight on my own. As a result, instead of walking with gratitude in the opportunities God has given me, I dread them. Rather than rejoicing over the open door I've been praying for, I'm wishing it was for anyone but me. I pray for God to provide, and when He does, instead of walking through those doors with confidence, I believe that I'm unqualified.

Are you waiting on a fresh outpouring from the Lord? Do you feel dry, burnt out, or empty? Maybe you've given so much you have nothing left, and you've fought so hard you've run out of ammo. Somewhere along the way, you got distracted, discouraged, or disconnected. You stopped spending time in the Word, stopped leaning on friends for prayer, and lost the passion you once had for life. Maybe it was an active decision to walk away. You got tired of pleading with God to change your circumstances with no answer. Or maybe it was a slow fade. You looked up and realized you were far from where you once were or wanted to be.

Reaching rock bottom, or just recognizing you're at a place where you want a major change, is actually something to celebrate—because this is where God can completely pour into you with a fresh oil that won't just fill you, it will overflow. The Bible says anyone who comes to Him can receive His outpouring. Sister, He's not holding out on you.

Heavenly Father, thank You for being the well that never runs dry. I've been wrestling with fear that if I keep pouring myself out, I'll end up empty. I want to give so generously that others seek You as their source too. Increase my faith and give me eyes to see who I can serve with the provision You've given me. In Jesus' name, amen.

Receive what He has for you

86

Live Expecting a Miracle

Then David said to the Philistine, "You come to me
with a sword and with a spear and with a javelin, but
I come to you in the name of the LORD of hosts, the
God of the armies of Israel, whom you have defied."

1 Samuel 17:45

I remember a season that felt like everything that could go wrong *did* go wrong. I woke each morning feeling so discouraged I could barely function. I had just gotten diagnosed with depression, and I tried a prescribed medication that would either make things "much better" or "much worse." (It made them *much* worse.) I felt so . . . *defeated*. Like I'd given my all, but it wasn't enough, and no matter how hard I fought, I'd always lose.

When you hear someone talk about "God's plan," you probably picture a life of success, influence, and abundance. At least I did. So facing giants that look about ready to take you out can make you feel incredibly far from it, right? If you're discouraged today by your latest setback, curveball, or full-blown battle, I want to challenge you to think outside the box. I want you to do something only possible through faith: to live expecting a miracle.

The Lord has already equipped you with everything you need to defeat the giants in front of you, and it has nothing to do with your skill, success, or qualification. You just need obedience and radical faith. So stop putting the dream, mission, or calling He's placed on your heart on the back burner because you don't know how it's all going to come together. When you have no choice but to hope for a miracle, you might actually have the opportunity to see one come to fruition.

In my difficult season the Lord reminded me of the story of David defeating Goliath. Goliath was intimidating, qualified, equipped, and the clear favorite in this battle. But David had faith. He trusted God could do the impossible, the unthinkable—that God could cause a miracle to happen. And David watched God supernaturally lead him to victory.

If David had backed down from the call, overwhelmed by the obvious physical disadvantage—if he had seen what everyone else assumed would be the outcome—he would have never experienced God's miraculous power that delivered Him. So step up to the plate today, friend, expectant of a miracle. Watch God show up for you.

Heavenly Father, help me surrender my desire to always get it "right" and simply walk in the direction You're calling me. Fear of failure has been keeping me from being fully obedient to what You're asking me to step into. I trust that You will redirect my steps toward Your perfect plan, and I ask for peace as You guide me through the unknown. In Jesus' name, amen.

87

Don't Let Fear Hold You Back

For God gave us a spirit not of fear.

2 Timothy 1:7

When the Lord told me to share my story of single motherhood on social media, I was terrified. My mind raced. *What will people think of me? What if they judge me? Or criticize me? Or ask for details I'm not ready to share?* I spent weeks trying to "perfect" the video—all because I was paralyzed by fear. It wasn't until I was crying out to the Lord, asking Him to show me what was next, that He convicted me. He'd already told me what to do. I was just dragging my feet. The resistance I felt was fueled by the Enemy, because sharing my story would change the trajectory of my life, and the Enemy would rather keep me stuck in fear.

Did you know that fear of any kind can simply be rebuked since it's not from God? Maybe God has instructed you to do something you've never done before, and you're dragging your feet, trying to "perfect" it before you start. Each time you get close to being ready, you decide something else needs a little more work, or you need more time, money, and so on. But deep down, you know you're secretly just terrified to fail. Believe me, I get it.

Sometimes it feels easier to have faith in your own failure, because at least that's something you can "control." You can easily go down a self-sabotage spiral, like I did with my social media announcement—feeling like you'd rather fail than go all in on God's plan. It was so easy for me to tell myself I didn't want to be irresponsible and jump into something the Lord had called me to without thoroughly preparing for it. Sound familiar?

But don't let a fear of failure be an excuse for keeping you stuck. God has so much more for you! It's vitally important to call out fear for what it is and ask God to reveal where it's holding you back—because if you can rebuke fear, you can walk by faith. God will reward that faith with grace and redirect you if needed. So release your desire to know exactly what's going to happen next and put your faith in the One who does.

When I rebuked the Enemy and the fear he was tempting me to stay in and shared my story publicly, guess what? I received overwhelming confirmation that sharing it mattered, and suddenly all the resistance I'd felt made sense. I heard from so many women that my story resonated with and encouraged them, and that my journey gave them hope for God's plan at work in their own lives. If I had chosen to stay bound by fear instead of walking by faith, I would have missed a huge opportunity to give God glory.

Heavenly Father, thank You for Your permission and authority to rebuke the fear the Enemy has tried to paralyze me with. I want to obey You, and to do a good job at what You're calling me into. Help me to be confident in Your power, and give me courage to step outside of my comfort zone to walk in Your plan. In Jesus' name, amen.

88
Stay Connected to the Vine

"I am the vine; you are the branches. Whoever abides in me and I in him, he it is that bears much fruit, for apart from me you can do nothing."

John 15:5

When I'm spending time in the Word every day, following the Holy Spirit's leading and not my own flesh, it almost feels like I'm having an out-of-body experience. There's a peace and joy that flows from me that feels supernatural. And it starts affecting others.

For instance, I recently texted a friend a word of encouragement, and they responded with, "How did you know I needed that after the news I heard just a minute ago?" I didn't. But the Holy Spirit did.

My pastor, Henry Seeley, once said, "Fruitfulness is the result of faithfulness." When we're connected to the vine, God helps us say and do exactly what someone else needs. The fruit we bear isn't a trophy for how hard we've worked. Instead, it's an overflow from the secret place where God works in and through us. God is doing His work, and He just asks us to be faithful. We aren't called to be the vine; we're called to stay connected to the vine. What blooms from there—the fruit you'll see in your life—will be an outgrowth of this source.

In John 15, Jesus said that apart from God, we can do nothing. We can try to make things happen on our own. We can get really good at being busy or looking productive. We can make long to-do lists and sign up for every volunteer opportunity, filling our calendars with stuff. But if we aren't connected to God, all of these "good" things can just distract us from His plan. They can take our focus off our calling, and lead to "results" but no actual fruit.

Bearing fruit is your calling. God will lead you through situations to produce a certain fruit in you—whether that's kindness, gentleness, self-control, or another aspect of the fruit of the Spirit—to give you what you'll need for what He's leading you to next.

Stay connected to the true vine, and watch God produce fruit that makes a kingdom impact. What an amazing thing to be a part of!

Heavenly Father, thank You for allowing me to simply stay connected to You in order to bear fruit. Help me to remember this when I'm striving to do so in my own strength. I don't want to spend any more time on my own plans that aren't aligned with the fullness You have for me. In Jesus' name, amen.

89

The Gift of Community

Two are better than one, because they have a good return for their labor: If either of them falls down, one can help the other up.

Ecclesiastes 4:9–10 NIV

I had no idea when I moved to Tennessee and became roommates with Enaka just how important community would be. I'm the oldest of eight siblings, so I grew up with a big family, and we're really close. My family has been such a huge source of support for me and Harv through a lot of our ups and downs. But my experience with Enaka and the church community I found in my new home state was overwhelming and completely unexpected. Why did these people who had no prior connection to me, who had nothing to gain from pouring into me—why did they love me so well?

During a season where I was at a crossroads in my faith, asking God why I was walking in my personal nightmare of divorce and single motherhood—He showed up. Not in the way I expected. He didn't reconcile my marriage right away or change my situation like I had pleaded with Him to. But He sent people. People who were truly the hands and feet of Jesus and displayed His love like I'd never experienced.

The coolest part was, as these people showed up with an encouraging word, groceries, or just to check in on me, they always gave me exactly what I needed. This wasn't just confirmation for *me* that God heard me. It was confirmation for *them* that God was using them so intentionally. Maybe God wasn't just allowing me to walk through a trial to teach me something, but to equip and use others to be His hands and feet at the same time.

I started the Abundantly More Community because as I shared my story on social media, the most common comment I received was "I wish I had community like that." I prayed and heard the Lord say, "Connect them with each other." So in 2021, I created a virtual community where we could all pray for, encourage, and uplift each other. Since then, I've watched thousands of strangers become sisters, and I've seen women who doubted their purpose walk it out in boldness. The power of Christ-centered community is life-changing. I can't encourage you enough to get plugged into your local church, and, of course, come join AMC to experience this transformation for yourself!

Friend, you have a life-changing, breakthrough-bringing purpose. I believe there are no coincidences with God and that He places people exactly where He needs them, at exactly the right time—allowing us to be a part of a plan bigger than we could imagine. Don't undermine the role your obedience plays in someone else's breakthrough or how God will use others in your own!

Thank You, Lord, for putting exactly the right people in my life to bring Your amazing plan to fruition. Open my eyes to see how You're provided abundantly for me through these friends and strangers. Help me to see how I can be the hands and feet of Jesus for others. In Jesus' name, amen.

90

There Is More in Store

God can do anything, you know—far more than you
could ever imagine or guess or request in your wildest
dreams! He does it not by pushing us around but by
working within us, his Spirit deeply and gently within us.

Ephesians 3:20 (The Message)

Friend, I'm so honored you've spent these ninety days with me, and I
hope you are encouraged to seek God's abundance for you in every
circumstance. Abundance isn't about getting what you want, having
your prayers answered a certain way, or stocking up on material
things. Don't think of abundance as a result. . . . Think of it as a
reminder. A reminder that God can and will do more than our minds
can comprehend. It will be so supernatural, there's no way you could
take credit for the results yourself. So don't let your current situation determine the level of your faith, but trust that your faith and
obedience to His call will lead to something so much better than
you could imagine.

What I love about The Message's translation of today's scripture is the way it emphasizes *how* God will accomplish "abundantly
more"—by working *within* you. Yes, I know the temptation is to stress
or strive for what's next. Can I encourage you to surrender instead?

I often find myself praying that God will use me for "more," and
while I believe that is part of His plan, what He often convicts me of

is desiring what He'll do *through* me more than what He wants to do *in* me. Don't fall into that trap! Draw near to Him, and let what He does *through* you be a natural overflow of your intimacy with Him.

Sister, I want to encourage you to remember that any moment of doubt, discomfort, or discouragement you encounter—it's not forever! Breakthrough is coming. God is making a way for abundance you can only prepare for in the valley. Galatians 6:9 says you *will* reap a harvest—if you do not give up.

I can't wait for you to experience God's abundant plan for your life and see what God does in and through you. Don't be surprised if you suddenly start seeing Ephesians 3:20 or "abundantly more" signs everywhere.

Take a second to thank Him for His mercy when you do!

Thank You, Lord, for showing how our temporary struggles won't last forever, but Your love and goodness do. Help me to walk with confidence in the fullness You have for me and to keep my eyes fixed on You as You prepare me for it. Give me the confidence to walk in my purpose and use my gifts for Your glory. In Jesus' name, amen.

GOD HAS ABUNDANTLY MORE IN STORE

About the Author

Sarah Grace Hallas is a ministry leader, Bible study teacher, and Christ-centered business coach for entrepreneurs. She encourages others in their faith on her TikTok and social media accounts by regularly sharing a real, behind-the-scenes look at her life and journey through motherhood and navigating life's ups and downs. Through her Abundantly More Community, she provides regular encouragement, live video devotions, opportunities to connect and grow in community with like-minded women, and other resources for those wanting to grow more confident in their faith and to walk in the fullness God has for them.

Subscribe to Sarah's newsletter and join the Abundantly More Community to receive biblical truth and encouragement to equip and empower you to walk in God's plan for your life!

www.AbundantlyMoreCommunity.com
TikTok + Instagram: @SarahGraceHallas